Garman

28
$2⁷⁸

HEAT ENERGY

Anthea Maton
Former NSTA National Coordinator
Project Scope, Sequence, Coordination
Washington, DC

Jean Hopkins
Science Instructor and Department Chairperson
John H. Wood Middle School
San Antonio, Texas

Susan Johnson
Professor of Biology
Ball State University
Muncie, Indiana

David LaHart
Senior Instructor
Florida Solar Energy Center
Cape Canaveral, Florida

Maryanna Quon Warner
Science Instructor
Del Dios Middle School
Escondido, California

Jill D. Wright
Professor of Science Education
Director of International Field Programs
University of Pittsburgh
Pittsburgh, Pennsylvania

Prentice Hall
Englewood Cliffs, New Jersey
Needham, Massachusetts

Prentice Hall Science
Heat Energy

Student Text and Annotated Teacher's Edition
Laboratory Manual
Teacher's Resource Package
Teacher's Desk Reference
Computer Test Bank
Teaching Transparencies
Product Testing Activities
Computer Courseware
Video and Interactive Video

The illustration on the cover, rendered by David Schleinkofer, is called a thermogram. The light colors show areas where heat is being lost.

Credits begin on page 88.

SECOND EDITION

ISBN 0-13-400698-4

10   97 96

Prentice Hall
A Division of Simon & Schuster
Englewood Cliffs, New Jersey 07632

STAFF CREDITS

Editorial:	Harry Bakalian, Pamela E. Hirschfeld, Maureen Grassi, Robert P. Letendre, Elisa Mui Eiger, Lorraine Smith-Phelan, Christine A. Caputo
Design:	AnnMarie Roselli, Carmela Pereira, Susan Walrath, Leslie Osher, Art Soares
Production:	Suse F. Bell, Joan McCulley, Elizabeth Torjussen, Christina Burghard
Photo Research:	Libby Forsyth, Emily Rose, Martha Conway
Publishing Technology:	Andrew Grey Bommarito, Deborah Jones, Monduane Harris, Michael Colucci, Gregory Myers, Cleasta Wilburn
Marketing:	Andrew Socha, Victoria Willows
Pre-Press Production:	Laura Sanderson, Kathryn Dix, Denise Herckenrath
Manufacturing:	Rhett Conklin, Gertrude Szyferblatt

Consultants

Kathy French	National Science Consultant
Jeannie Dennard	National Science Consultant
Brenda Underwood	National Science Consultant
Janelle Conarton	National Science Consultant

Contributing Writers

Linda Densman
Science Instructor
Hurst, TX

Linda Grant
Former Science Instructor
Weatherford, TX

Heather Hirschfeld
Science Writer
Durham, NC

Marcia Mungenast
Science Writer
Upper Montclair, NJ

Michael Ross
Science Writer
New York City, NY

Content Reviewers

Dan Anthony
Science Mentor
Rialto, CA

John Barrow
Science Instructor
Pomona, CA

Leslie Bettencourt
Science Instructor
Harrisville, RI

Carol Bishop
Science Instructor
Palm Desert, CA

Dan Bohan
Science Instructor
Palm Desert, CA

Steve M. Carlson
Science Instructor
Milwaukie, OR

Larry Flammer
Science Instructor
San Jose, CA

Steve Ferguson
Science Instructor
Lee's Summit, MO

Robin Lee Harris Freedman
Science Instructor
Fort Bragg, CA

Edith H. Gladden
Former Science Instructor
Philadelphia, PA

Vernita Marie Graves
Science Instructor
Tenafly, NJ

Jack Grube
Science Instructor
San Jose, CA

Emiel Hamberlin
Science Instructor
Chicago, IL

Dwight Kertzman
Science Instructor
Tulsa, OK

Judy Kirschbaum
Science/Computer Instructor
Tenafly, NJ

Kenneth L. Krause
Science Instructor
Milwaukie, OR

Ernest W. Kuehl, Jr.
Science Instructor
Bayside, NY

Mary Grace Lopez
Science Instructor
Corpus Christi, TX

Warren Maggard
Science Instructor
PeWee Valley, KY

Della M. McCaughan
Science Instructor
Biloxi, MS

Stanley J. Mulak
Former Science Instructor
Jensen Beach, FL

Richard Myers
Science Instructor
Portland, OR

Carol Nathanson
Science Mentor
Riverside, CA

Sylvia Neivert
Former Science Instructor
San Diego, CA

Jarvis VNC Pahl
Science Instructor
Rialto, CA

Arlene Sackman
Science Instructor
Tulare, CA

Christine Schumacher
Science Instructor
Pikesville, MD

Suzanne Steinke
Science Instructor
Towson, MD

Len Svinth
Science Instructor/ Chairperson
Petaluma, CA

Elaine M. Tadros
Science Instructor
Palm Desert, CA

Joyce K. Walsh
Science Instructor
Midlothian, VA

Steve Weinberg
Science Instructor
West Hartford, CT

Charlene West, PhD
Director of Curriculum
Rialto, CA

John Westwater
Science Instructor
Medford, MA

Glenna Wilkoff
Science Instructor
Chesterfield, OH

Edee Norman Wiziecki
Science Instructor
Urbana, IL

Teacher Advisory Panel

Beverly Brown
Science Instructor
Livonia, MI

James Burg
Science Instructor
Cincinnati, OH

Karen M. Cannon
Science Instructor
San Diego, CA

John Eby
Science Instructor
Richmond, CA

Elsie M. Jones
Science Instructor
Marietta, GA

Michael Pierre McKereghan
Science Instructor
Denver, CO

Donald C. Pace, Sr.
Science Instructor
Reisterstown, MD

Carlos Francisco Sainz
Science Instructor
National City, CA

William Reed
Science Instructor
Indianapolis, IN

Multicultural Consultant

Steven J. Rakow
Associate Professor
University of Houston— Clear Lake
Houston, TX

English as a Second Language (ESL) Consultants

Jaime Morales
Bilingual Coordinator
Huntington Park, CA

Pat Hollis Smith
Former ESL Instructor
Beaumont, TX

Reading Consultant

Larry Swinburne
Director
Swinburne Readability Laboratory

CONTENTS

Activity Bank/Reference Section

Features

CONCEPT MAPPING

Throughout your study of science, you will learn a variety of terms, facts, figures, and concepts. Each new topic you encounter will provide its own collection of words and ideas—which, at times, you may think seem endless. But each of the ideas within a particular topic is related in some way to the others. No concept in science is isolated. Thus it will help you to understand the topic if you see the whole picture; that is, the interconnectedness of all the individual terms and ideas. This is a much more effective and satisfying way of learning than memorizing separate facts.

Actually, this should be a rather familiar process for you. Although you may not think about it in this way, you analyze many of the elements in your daily life by looking for relationships or connections. For example, when you look at a collection of flowers, you may divide them into groups: roses, carnations, and daisies. You may then associate colors with these flowers: red, pink, and white. The general topic is flowers. The subtopic is types of flowers. And the colors are specific terms that describe flowers. A topic makes more sense and is more easily understood if you understand how it is broken down into individual ideas and how these ideas are related to one another and to the entire topic.

It is often helpful to organize information visually so that you can see how it all fits together. One technique for describing related ideas is called a **concept map**. In a concept map, an idea is represented by a word or phrase enclosed in a box. There are several ideas in any concept map. A connection between two ideas is made with a line. A word or two that describes the connection is written on or near the line. The general topic is located at the top of the map. That topic is then broken down into subtopics, or more specific ideas, by branching lines. The most specific topics are located at the bottom of the map.

To construct a concept map, first identify the important ideas or key terms in the chapter or section. Do not try to include too much information. Use your judgment as to what is really important. Write the general topic at the top of your map. Let's use an example to help illustrate this process. Suppose you decide that the key terms in a section you are reading are School, Living Things, Language Arts, Subtraction, Grammar, Mathematics, Experiments, Papers, Science, Addition, Novels. The general topic is School. Write and enclose this word in a box at the top of your map.

SCHOOL

Now choose the subtopics—Language Arts, Science, Mathematics. Figure out how they are related to the topic. Add these words to your map. Continue this procedure until you have included all the important ideas and terms. Then use lines to make the appropriate connections between ideas and terms. Don't forget to write a word or two on or near the connecting line to describe the nature of the connection.

Do not be concerned if you have to redraw your map (perhaps several times!) before you show all the important connections clearly. If, for example, you write papers for Science as well as for Language Arts, you may want to place these two subjects next to each other so that the lines do not overlap.

One more thing you should know about concept mapping: Concepts can be correctly mapped in many different ways. In fact, it is unlikely that any two people will draw identical concept maps for a complex topic. Thus there is no one correct concept map for any topic! Even

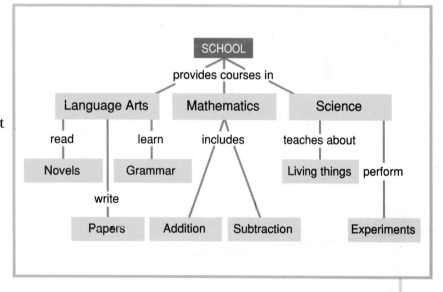

though your concept map may not match those of your classmates, it will be correct as long as it shows the most important concepts and the clear relationships among them. Your concept map will also be correct if it has meaning to you and if it helps you understand the material you are reading. A concept map should be so clear that if some of the terms are erased, the missing terms could easily be filled in by following the logic of the concept map.

HEAT ENERGY

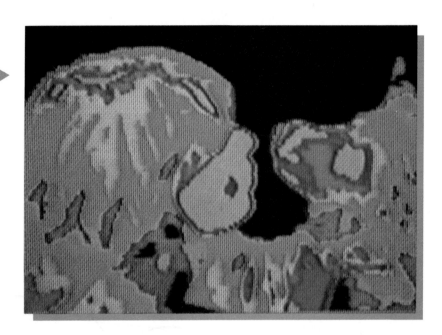

This colorful photograph of a girl and her dog is a special kind of image called a thermogram. Notice that the dog's nose appears dark blue in the thermogram. Does this mean that the dog's nose is hot or cold?

Fire is useful when it is properly controlled. However, it is also quite dangerous. An out-of-control forest fire can be extremely destructive.

The colorful picture above is not a cartoon or a computer graphic. It is a thermogram of a young girl and her pet dog. A thermogram (from *thermo-* meaning heat and *-gram* meaning something recorded) is an image formed by the invisible heat given off by an object. In this thermogram, the hottest areas are bright and the coolest areas are dark. Doctors can use thermograms to determine whether parts of the body are functioning properly.

Thermograms illustrate only one way in which heat is important in our lives. Heat is also important because of its many uses. Thousands of years ago, early humans discovered fire and began using it to heat their cave dwellings and to cook their food. Today, central heating and cooling systems make our homes, schools, and office buildings comfortable places in which to live and work. Heat engines—from steam engines to modern

CHAPTERS

1 What Is Heat?   **2** Uses of Heat

gasoline engines—help make our work easier. But heat can also damage the environment if we are not careful.

What exactly is heat? You will find the answer to that question in this textbook. You will also learn about the many applications of heat in your daily life.

As this painting of cowboys gathered around an open fire in the Old West illustrates, the ability to use fire for heating and cooking was one of the most important discoveries in human history.

Burning coals glow reddish yellow. In the heart of the fire, the hottest coals glow white hot.

Discovery *Activity*

In Hot Water

1. Fill three bowls with water. Put cold water in one bowl, warm water in the second bowl, and hot (but not too hot to touch) water in the third bowl.

2. Now place one hand in the cold water and one hand in the hot water.

3. After about a minute, place both hands in the warm water. Does the temperature of the warm water feel the same to both hands?

   ■ Is using your hands a good way to measure heat? Could a scientist measure heat in this way?

   ■ What does this experiment tell you about the relationship between heat and temperature?

What Is Heat?

Guide for Reading

After you read the following sections, you will be able to

1–1 Heat: A Form of Energy
- Describe how scientists discovered that heat is a form of energy.

1–2 Temperature and Heat
- Define temperature in terms of the kinetic energy of molecules.

1–3 Measuring Heat
- Describe how heat can be measured indirectly.

1–4 Heat and Phase Changes
- Explain how a transfer of heat energy causes a phase change.

1–5 Thermal Expansion
- Explain why thermal expansion occurs.
- Describe some practical applications of thermal expansion.

Alone and lost in a snowy, barren wilderness, a man wanders in search of warmth and shelter. He is rapidly losing his body heat to the much colder surroundings. Although he is dressed in layers of thick clothing, he cannot hold enough heat to keep his body functioning. He is slowly freezing to death. If he could find some wood to burn, the fire would produce enough heat to warm him. But he is surrounded by snow and ice!

This exciting adventure story, called "To Build a Fire," was written by the American author Jack London. But it is more than just a thrilling tale of a man's struggle to survive in the wilderness. It is also a story about heat and the attempt to understand and control it. In this sense, it is a story about scientific knowledge.

An understanding of heat and the many roles it plays in the lives of real people is important to you, too. Who knows? Someday this knowledge may even save your life. As you read this chapter you will find out what heat is, how it is measured, and how it affects the world around you. As for the man in the snow, you will have to read the story to find out what happened to him!

Journal *Activity*

You and Your World Try to remember a situation when you were really cold or really hot. How did you feel? What did you do to make yourself warmer or cooler? Describe your feelings and actions in your journal. After reading this chapter, is there anything you would do differently?

◀ *Lost in a snowy wilderness*

1–1 Heat: A Form of Energy

An open fire casts a warm glow on your face and the faces of your fellow campers as you toast marshmallows over the flames. Sitting near an open fire, you know that the fire gives off **heat.** You might be tempted to think that heat is some kind of substance flowing from the fire, through the air, and into your marshmallow. Actually, that is just what eighteenth-century scientists believed. They thought that heat was an invisible, weightless fluid capable of flowing from hotter objects to colder ones. They called this substance caloric.

In 1798, the American scientist Benjamin Thompson (who moved to England after the American Revolution and became known as Count Rumford) challenged the caloric theory. Rumford had noticed that when holes were drilled in cannon barrels, the barrels and the drills became hot. Heat was being produced. Rumford decided to find out how. He designed an experiment to test his observation. A cannon barrel to be drilled was first placed in a box filled with water. After several hours of drilling, the water began to boil. The water boiled as long as the drilling continued. Rumford concluded that it was

A CTIVITY

WRITING

Rumford and Joule

The investigations of Count Rumford and James Prescott Joule illustrate the importance of careful observation and experimentation. Using books and other reference materials in the library, find out more about these two scientists, their experiments, and their contributions to the understanding of heat. Write a report of your findings.

Figure 1–1 *At one time people believed that the heat from a fire was a substance called caloric. Heat is now known to be a form of energy related to the motion of molecules.*

the action of drilling, not a flow of caloric, that was producing heat. Since drilling represents work being done and energy is the ability to do work, energy and heat must be related. Rumford concluded that heat must be a form of energy.

Molecules in Motion

Forty years after Count Rumford's experiment, the British scientist James Prescott Joule investigated the relationship between heat and motion. He performed a series of experiments which supported the idea that objects in motion can produce heat. The amount of heat produced depends on the amount of motion. You have probably already noticed this effect in your everyday life. Rub your hands together rapidly. What happens? Your hands feel warmer. Similarly, sliding too quickly down a rope can produce a "rope burn." These examples demonstrate that motion produces heat. Can you think of any other examples?

Other scientists working at the same time as Joule knew that energy is needed to set an object in motion. They also knew that matter is made up of tiny particles called **molecules** (MAHL-ih-kyoolz), which are always in motion. Combining these facts with the results of the experiments of Rumford and Joule, scientists correctly concluded that heat is a form of energy and that it is somehow related to the motion of molecules. **In fact, heat is a form of energy caused by the internal motion of molecules of matter.**

Activity Bank

May the Force (of Friction) Be With You, p.74

Figure 1–2 *Heated molecules (right) move faster and are farther apart than cooler molecules (left).*

Figure 1–3 *Melting ice cream bars provide these children with a messy lesson: Heat is transferred from warmer objects to colder objects.*

Heat Transfer

Try holding an ice cube in your hand for a short time. What happens? After several seconds, you notice that your hand begins to feel cold and the ice cube begins to melt. You might think that the coldness of the ice cube is moving from the ice cube to your hand. But there is no such thing as "coldness." Cold is simply the absence of heat. So it must be heat that is moving. The ice cube in your hand is melting because heat is moving from your hand to the ice cube. If you have ever accidentally touched a hot pan, you have discovered for yourself (most likely in a painful way) that heat energy moves from a warmer object to a cooler object. The heat moves from the hot pan, through the handle, to your hand!

The movement of heat from a warmer object to a cooler one is called **heat transfer.** There are three methods of heat transfer. **Heat energy is transferred by conduction, convection, and radiation.** Let's see how each of these processes takes place.

CONDUCTION In the process of **conduction** (kuhn-DUHK-shuhn), heat is transferred through a substance, or from one substance to another, by the

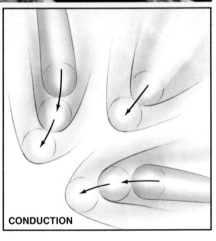

CONDUCTION

Figure 1–4 *Heat transfer by conduction involves the direct contact of molecules. As fast-moving molecules collide with slow-moving molecules, heat energy is transferred from the faster molecules to the slower molecules. Conduction by direct contact is one reason this lizard steps gingerly on a hot rock.*

Figure 1–5 *Why do several layers of clothing keep these children better insulated from the cold than a single layer of clothing?*

direct contact of molecules. All molecules are constantly in motion. Fast-moving molecules have more heat energy than slow-moving molecules.

When fast-moving molecules collide with slow-moving molecules, heat energy is transferred from the faster molecules to the slower molecules, causing the slower molecules to move faster. Now these molecules have enough energy to collide with other slow-moving molecules. This process is repeated over and over. In this way, heat energy is transferred from molecule to molecule throughout a substance. Because all matter is made of molecules, conduction can take place in solids, liquids, and gases. But conduction takes place best in solids, because the molecules of a solid are in direct contact with one another.

Some substances conduct heat better and more rapidly than other substances. These substances are good **conductors** of heat. Metals, such as iron and aluminum, are good heat conductors. Silver is one of the best conductors of heat. Copper is another good conductor of heat. Why do you think the bottoms of pots and pans are often made of copper?

Substances that do not conduct heat easily are called **insulators.** Glass, wood, plastic, and rubber are examples of good insulators. Why should the handles of pots and pans be made of wood or plastic instead of iron or aluminum?

ACTIVITY

DISCOVERING

Heat and Electricity

Good conductors of heat are usually also good conductors of electricity.

1. Set up a battery, a light bulb, wires, and alligator clips according to your teacher's directions.

2. Test different materials to find out if they are good conductors of electricity. For example, you might test a rubber band, a metal paper clip, a plastic spoon, and a wooden pencil. To test each object, place it between the clips on the free ends of the wires. If the material conducts electricity, the bulb will light.

■ Which of the materials you tested conduct electricity?

■ Which materials would probably conduct heat easily? Which would not?

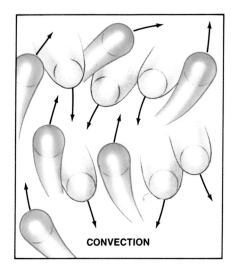

CONVECTION

Figure 1–6 *Heat transfer by convection involves the motion of molecules in currents in liquids and gases. Heated molecules speed up and spread out, causing the warmer part of the liquid or gas to become less dense than the cooler part. The heated portion rises, creating currents that carry heat. How do hot-air balloons make use of convection to float high above Earth's surface?*

A<small>CTIVITY</small>

Using Convection Currents

Suppose you want to let air into a stuffy room. Should you open the window from the top or the bottom if the outside temperature is warmer than the room temperature? What if the outside temperature is cooler than the room temperature? Draw a diagram to explain your answers.

■ With an adult's permission, determine if your explanations are correct.

Air is also a good insulator. That is why the best way to stay warm in extremely cold weather is to wear several layers of clothing. Layers of clothing will trap air close to your body and prevent the loss of body heat.

CONVECTION   Heat transfer by **convection** (kuhn-VEHK-shuhn) takes place in liquids and gases. Heat energy is transferred through liquids and gases by means of up-and-down movements called convection currents. When a liquid or gas is heated, the molecules begin to move faster. (They have more energy as a result of being heated.) As the molecules move faster, they move farther apart. This means that the heated liquid or gas is now less dense than the surrounding liquid or gas. The less-dense liquid or gas rises, carrying heat with it.

Warm air near the surface of the Earth is heated by the Earth and becomes less dense than the cooler air above it. The warm air tends to rise. Hang gliders and soaring birds rely on updrafts of warm air to help keep them aloft. Because cooler air is denser than warmer air, it tends to sink, just as a dense rock sinks in water. As warm air rises and cool air sinks, convection currents are formed. These currents transfer heat throughout the Earth's atmosphere and contribute to the Earth's weather. Convection currents are also formed in the Earth's oceans as warm water rises to the surface and cold water sinks to the bottom.

RADIATION Heat energy is transferred through empty space by **radiation** (ray-dee-AY-shuhn). Heat from the sun reaches the Earth by means of radiation. The heat energy is in the form of invisible light called infrared radiation. Other familiar forms of heat transfer by radiation include the heat you can feel around an open fire or a candle flame, the heat near a hot stove, and the heat given off by an electric heater. Now can you explain why you can toast marshmallows over a fire even if the flames do not touch the marshmallows?

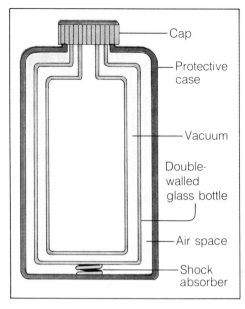

Figure 1–7 *A thermos bottle keeps liquids hot or cold by preventing heat transfer by conduction, convection, or radiation. The glass bottle reduces conduction. The air space between the bottles, which is a partial vacuum, prevents heat transfer by convection because there are so few air molecules to carry the heat. A silvered coating on the surface of the bottle prevents heat transfer by radiation. Why is the cap usually made of plastic?*

Figure 1–8 *Radiation is the transfer of heat energy in the form of invisible infrared rays. How is radiation from the sun related to the heating of the Earth?*

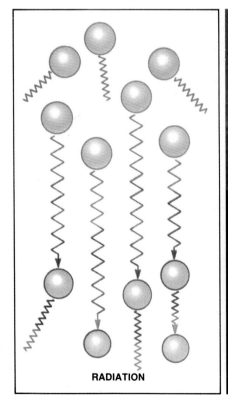

RADIATION

ACTIVITY

DISCOVERING

Heat Loss

Make a list of places in your home or school where heat may be escaping to the outside. Determine whether the heat loss is due to conduction, convection, or radiation.

■ How can the heat loss from the building be reduced?

PROBLEM Solving

Too Hot to Fly

One day in July, passenger jets at the airport in Phoenix, Arizona, were grounded. The problem? The air temperature—a sizzling 50°C—was just too hot for the planes to get off the ground! The planes had to wait several hours until the temperature dropped a few degrees before they could take off.

Applying Concepts

Why do you think the planes were unable to take off in the hot air? (*Hint:* When a plane is moving fast enough to take off, air moving past the plane's wings normally provides enough "lift" for the plane to get off the ground. But what happens to air when it is heated?)

1–1 Section Review

1. What is heat? How did the experiments of Rumford and Joule help contribute to an understanding of the nature of heat?
2. What are the three methods of heat transfer? How does each method work?
3. What are molecules? What factors caused scientists to make a connection between heat and the motion of molecules?

Connection—*You and Your World*

4. Identify the method of heat transfer illustrated by each of the following: an egg cooking in a frying pan; a warm air mass bringing a change in weather; the wire of an electric appliance becoming hot; heat from a fireplace warming a room.

1-2 Temperature and Heat

If a weather forecaster predicts temperatures between 30°C and 35°C, you know you can expect a hot day. Many people—perhaps even you—think that temperature and heat are the same thing. But they are not. Temperature and heat are related, but they are not the same. In order to understand the difference between temperature and heat, you will need to look more closely at how energy and the motion of molecules are related.

Kinetic Energy

Count Rumford observed that heat was produced when a hole was drilled in a cannon barrel. James Prescott Joule observed that objects in motion produce heat. In both cases, work is being done. What do you think of when you hear the word work? You may think of doing chores, such as washing dishes or raking leaves. Or perhaps going to work in an office comes to mind. But when scientists speak of work, they are referring to a force (a push or a pull) acting on an object and causing it to move. A moving hammer can do work by hitting a nail and driving it into a piece of wood. Moving objects can do work because they have energy. Energy of motion is called **kinetic** (kih-NEHT-ihk) **energy.** The faster an object moves, the more kinetic energy it has. So a fast-moving hammer can do more work than a slow-moving one. You can test this by hammering a nail

Figure 1–9 *Heat within the Earth increases the kinetic energy of water molecules so that they escape from the Earth as an eruption of hot water and steam. How does Old Faithful geyser in Yellowstone National Park, Wyoming, illustrate the relationship between heat and temperature?*

Figure 1–10 *Kinetic energy is defined as the energy of motion. How does the kinetic energy of the gazelles change when they are running from a predator that wants to eat them?*

Exploring Molecular Motion

1. Fill a beaker about two thirds full with water at or near room temperature.

2. Fill a second beaker about two thirds full with cold water. (You can use ice cubes to cool the water, but be sure to remove the ice before adding the cold water to the beaker.)

3. Using a medicine dropper, place one drop of dark food coloring on the surface of the water in each beaker. Do not stir. What changes do you see in each beaker? How quickly do the changes occur in each beaker?

■ How are your observations related to the effect of heat on the motion of molecules?

into a piece of wood. The faster you swing the hammer, the farther the nail is driven into the wood.

Like all moving objects, molecules have kinetic energy because of their motion. **Temperature is a measure of the average kinetic energy of molecules.** Adding heat to a substance increases the average kinetic energy of the molecules and causes a rise in temperature. Thus **temperature** is a measure of how hot or how cold something is. The higher the temperature of a substance, the faster the molecules in that substance are moving, on the average. Likewise, a lower temperature indicates that the molecules are moving more slowly. In which pot of water would most of the water molecules be moving faster—a pot at 90°C or one at 70°C?

Unlike temperature, heat depends on the mass of the substance present. For instance, 10 grams of water at 90°C have more heat energy than 5 grams of water at the same temperature. This means that if you were to spill hot water on your hand by accident, 10 grams of water at 90°C would produce a more severe burn than 5 grams of water at 90°C!

Measuring Temperature

You would not want to put your hand into a pot of boiling water to find out how hot the water is! And you might not always agree with someone else on how hot or how cold something is. So you need a safe and accurate way of measuring temperature. A **thermometer** is an instrument for measuring temperature. Most common thermometers consist of a thin tube filled with a liquid, usually alcohol or mercury. Remember that as a liquid is heated, its molecules move faster and farther apart. So as the liquid in a thermometer gets warmer, it expands and rises in the tube. The opposite happens as the liquid gets cooler. The molecules move slower and closer together. The liquid contracts and drops in the tube.

Along the tube of a thermometer is a set of numbers, called a scale, that allows you to read the temperature. The **Celsius scale** is used to measure

Figure 1–11 *At a temperature of −198.5°C, nitrogen gas becomes a liquid. A banana dipped in liquid nitrogen becomes so frozen it can be used to hammer a nail into a block of wood.*

Figure 1–12 *A comparison of the Celsius and Kelvin temperature scales is shown here. Notice that absolute zero is –273°C. Uranus, located farther from the sun than Earth, has temperatures near absolute zero.*

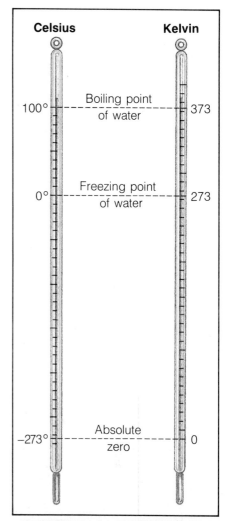

temperature in the metric system. The unit of temperature on the Celsius scale is the degree Celsius (°C). Water freezes at 0°C and boils at 100°C.

Another metric temperature scale often used by scientists is the **Kelvin scale.** On this scale, temperature is measured in units called kelvins (K). You can convert Celsius degrees to kelvins simply by adding 273 to the Celsius temperature. For example, if a thermometer reads 10°C, the same temperature on the Kelvin scale would be 273 + 10 = 283 K. A temperature of –5°C equals 268 K [273 + (–5)]. At what temperature does water freeze on the Kelvin scale? At what Kelvin temperature does water boil?

The main reason the Kelvin scale is useful to scientists is that the lowest reading on this scale, 0 K, is the lowest temperature that can be reached. This temperature is often called **absolute zero.** Scientists have now been able to reach a temperature only one millionth of a degree Celsius above absolute zero.

You may not have guessed that there is a lowest possible temperature. Recall that temperature is a measure of the energy of motion of molecules. What do you think happens at absolute zero?

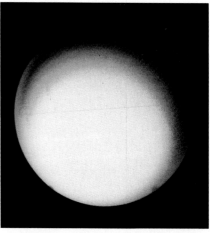

1–2 Section Review

1. What is temperature? What is the difference between temperature and heat?
2. How does a thermometer measure temperature?
3. What is the most common metric scale used to measure temperature? What temperature scale is most often used by scientists?
4. How would you convert a temperature in kelvins to degrees Celsius?

Critical Thinking—*Relating Concepts*

5. Do you think a temperature of absolute zero can ever be reached? Why or why not?

Activity Bank

One Hundred Degrees of Separation, p.75

CONNECTIONS

Suspended Animation

A concept once found only in science fiction has moved into the operating rooms of modern hospitals. In science fiction movies, astronauts embarking on a long space voyage are put into a state of "suspended animation" from which they can be revived when they reach their destination. Actually, this physical state is called hypothermic arrest (from the prefix *hypo-,* meaning lower than normal, and *-therm,* meaning heat). In hypothermic arrest, the heart stops beating and blood circulation comes to a halt. Hypothermic arrest is deadly under normal circumstances.

Today, hypothermic arrest is used in *medicine.* Doctors can cool the body of a patient to a state of near death in order to perform brain surgery without a flow of blood! A person can survive hypothermic arrest because the brain can survive longer without oxygen at low temperatures.

In 1990, surgeons at Columbia Presbyterian Medical Center in New York City used the procedure to correct an aneurysm (AN-yoo-rihz-uhm) in the brain of a 24-year-old man. In an aneurysm, the wall of a blood vessel puffs out like a little balloon. The ballooning blood vessel presses on the brain, causing paralysis and eventual death.

In the case of the patient at Columbia, the aneurysm was buried deep in the brain. A team of surgeons lowered the patient's temperature until his heart stopped. Then they drained his blood and repaired the aneurysm. Once the surgery was completed, blood was again allowed to flow through the patient's body, his temperature rose, and his heart began to beat. A week later, he left the hospital! A normally deadly process had saved his life.

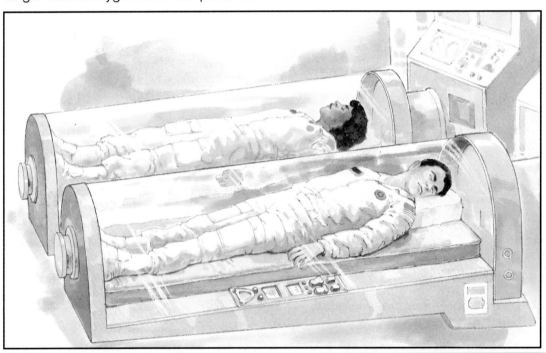

1–3 Measuring Heat

You know that when you cook soup or boil water, heat energy must be added to the liquid in order to raise its temperature. Heat energy is needed to set molecules in motion. Temperature is a measure of this molecular motion.

Heat cannot be measured directly. But changes in temperature—which can be measured directly—provide a way to measure heat indirectly. **An increase in temperature indicates that heat is being added. A decrease in temperature indicates that heat is being removed.**

Heat is measured in units called **calories.** One calorie (cal) is defined as the amount of heat needed to raise the temperature of 1 gram of water 1 degree Celsius. For example, to raise the temperature of 1 gram of water from 4°C to 5°C or from 20°C to 21°C, 1 calorie of heat is needed. Another unit that can be used to measure heat is the joule (J), named after James Prescott Joule. One calorie is equal to 4.19 joules (1 cal = 4.19 J).

Notice that the amount of heat needed for a given temperature change depends on the mass of the water being heated. For example, 10 calories of heat

Guide for Reading

Focus on this question as you read.

▶ *How can changes in temperature be used to measure heat indirectly?*

Figure 1–13 *Although heat cannot be measured directly, a change in temperature provides an indirect measurement of heat. Higher temperatures indicate more heat whereas lower temperatures indicate an absence of heat.*

TABLE OF SPECIFIC HEATS	
Substance	**Specific Heat (cal/g·°C)**
Air	0.25
Aluminum	0.22
Copper	0.09
Glass	0.20
Ice (–20°C to 0°C)	0.50
Iron	0.11
Mercury	0.03
Ocean water	0.93
Water	1.00
Wood	0.42

Figure 1–14 *According to this table of specific heats, which heats up more quickly: aluminum or mercury?*

will raise the temperature of 1 gram of water 10°C. If you had 10 grams of water instead of 1 gram, the same 10 calories would raise the temperature of the water only 1°C. How many calories would be needed to raise the temperature of 10 grams of water 10°C?

Specific Heat Capacity

Mass is not the only factor that determines temperature change. The same amount of heat will produce a different temperature change in different substances even if their masses are the same. That is because some substances absorb heat energy more readily than other substances.

The ability of a substance to absorb heat energy is called its **specific heat.** The specific heat of a substance is the number of calories needed to raise the temperature of 1 gram of that substance 1 degree Celsius. The specific heat of water is 1 calorie per gram per degree Celsius (1.00 cal/g·°C). This is high compared with the specific heats of most other substances.

The high specific heat of water explains why the climate near an ocean or a large lake is usually mild. Water tends to heat up slowly, but it also loses heat slowly. This slow heating and cooling tends to keep the climate near a large body of water relatively uniform.

Figure 1–14 lists the specific heat values of some other common substances. Specific heat is an important property because it can be used to help decide which substance should be used for a specific purpose. For example, you can see by looking at Figure 1–14 that the specific heat of aluminum is almost twice that of iron. That means that aluminum pots and pans hold about twice as much heat as pots and pans of the same mass made of iron.

Calculating Heat Energy

Specific heat can be used to calculate the amount of heat gained or lost by a substance. The heat gained or lost by a substance is equal to the product of its mass times the change in temperature (ΔT) times its specific heat. (The symbol Δ is the Greek letter delta; ΔT means change in temperature.)

Figure 1–15 *The calorimeter shown here can be used to measure the heat given off during a chemical reaction. What principle of heat transfer is the basis of operation of the calorimeter?*

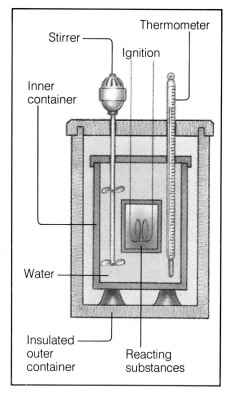

Heat gained or lost = Mass × ΔT × Specific heat

Within a closed container, the heat lost by one substance must equal the heat gained by another substance. A device that makes use of this principle is called a **calorimeter** (kal-uh-RIHM-uht-er). A calorimeter can be used to measure the heat given off in chemical reactions.

Figure 1–15 shows how a calorimeter is constructed. An insulated outer container surrounds an inner container filled with water. Inside the inner container is a chamber in which a chemical reaction takes place. Because the heat given off by the chemical reaction equals the heat gained by the water, the heat of the chemical reaction can be calculated. The temperature change, mass, and specific heat of the water must be known in order to make the calculation. For example, suppose the surrounding water has a mass of 300 grams. If the temperature of the

---

Sample Problem

How much heat is needed to raise the temperature of 4 grams of aluminum 5°C?

Solution

Step 1   Write the formula.

Step 2   Substitute given numbers and units.

Heat gained = Mass × ΔT × Specific heat

Heat gained = 4 g × 5°C × 0.22 cal/g·°C

Step 3   Solve for unknown variable.

Heat gained = 4.4 cal

Practice Problems

1. Calculate the heat lost by 10 g of copper if it is cooled from 35°C to 21°C.

2. Suppose that 10 grams of a certain substance gained 16.5 cal of heat when the temperature increased from 70°C to 85°C. What would be the specific heat of the substance?

water increases 5°C, the heat given off by the chemical reaction is equal to 300 g × 5°C × 1 cal/g·°C = 1500 calories. How much heat would be given off by a chemical reaction that raised the temperature of 150 grams of water 10°C?

Potential Energy

When does heat energy not cause a change in the temperature of a substance? The answer to this question is quite simple: when the heat energy is stored. Stored energy—in the form of heat or any other kind of energy—is called **potential** (poh-TEHN-shuhl) **energy.** Potential heat energy is present in chemical substances such as gasoline and other fuels. The stored heat energy is released when the fuels are burned, for example, in a car engine.

Foods also contain potential heat energy. The energy stored in foods can be measured in calories because when foods are "burned," they release heat energy. ("Burning" food in your body involves the process of respiration, in which food that is broken

Activity Bank

These "Fuelish" Things, p.76

Figure 1–16 *The stored, or potential, energy in rocket fuel provides the boost needed to launch a Space Shuttle. Stored energy in food provides a similar boost to you.*

down into sugar is combined with oxygen to release energy.) When sugars are burned in your body, heat energy needed to keep your body functioning is produced. The amount of heat a food gives off is indicated by the number of calories it contains. There is one big difference, however. "Food calories" are really kilocalories (kcal). And 1 kilocalorie is equal to 1000 calories. Food calories are usually written with a capital C to differentiate them from calories with a small c. So the next time you are on a diet, you can tell your friends that you are watching your kilocalories!

1–3 Section Review

1. How can heat be measured? What unit is used to measure heat?
2. What is specific heat? Why is it important?
3. What is a calorimeter? How does it work?

Critical Thinking—*Making Calculations*
4. Which would require more heat energy—raising the temperature of 100 grams of water from 40°C to 100°C or raising the temperature of 1000 grams of water from 80°C to 90°C? Show your calculations.

1–4 Heat and Phase Changes

Have you ever watched an ice cube melt in a glass of water? If so, have you been curious about why this happens? Heat always moves from a warm substance to a cooler substance. Because the water is warmer than the ice, heat moves from the water to the ice. As the ice absorbs heat, it melts, or changes into a liquid. Eventually all the solid ice will change into liquid water.

Matter can exist in three phases: solid, liquid, and gas. The physical change of matter from the solid phase (ice) to the liquid phase (water) is called a

Guide for Reading

Focus on this question as you read.

▶ *What causes a phase change?*

Figure 1–17 *Matter can exist in three phases. Which phases of matter can be observed in this photograph?*

Figure 1–18 *With the addition of heat, these water droplets will change phase and become gaseous water in the atmosphere. What term is used for the amount of heat needed to change a liquid to a gas?*

phase change. Matter can undergo several different phase changes. Phase changes occur when a solid becomes a liquid, which is called melting, and when a liquid becomes a solid, which is called freezing. The change of a liquid to a gas, or evaporation, and the change of a gas to a liquid, or condensation, are also phase changes.

What causes a phase change? **A change in phase requires a change in heat energy.** When ice melts and changes into water, energy in the form of heat is being absorbed by the ice. The energy is needed to overcome the forces of attraction that hold the water molecules together in the solid phase (ice). Where do you think the heat energy needed to melt the ice in a glass of water is coming from?

Heat of Fusion and Heat of Vaporization

The amount of heat needed to change 1 gram of a substance from the solid phase to the liquid phase is called **heat of fusion.** The heat of fusion of ice is 80 calories per gram (cal/g). This means that in order to melt 1 gram of ice, 80 calories of heat are needed. What do you think happens when 1 gram of liquid water changes into ice? You are right if you said that 80 calories of heat are lost by 1 gram of liquid water as it changes into ice. How much heat is needed to change 10 grams of ice into water?

The amount of heat needed to change 1 gram of a substance from the liquid phase to the gas phase is called **heat of vaporization.** The heat of vaporization of water is 540 calories per gram. This means that 540 calories of heat must be added to 1 gram of water in order to change it into steam. How much heat is needed to change 10 grams of water into steam? How much heat is given off if 10 grams of steam are condensed into water?

Melting, Freezing, and Boiling Points

In order for a substance to undergo a phase change, the substance must be at a certain temperature. The temperature at which a substance changes from the liquid phase to the solid phase is called its **freezing point.** The freezing point of water is 0°C. The temperature at which a substance changes from the solid phase to the liquid phase is its **melting point.** A substance's freezing point and melting point are the same. Can you explain why? The

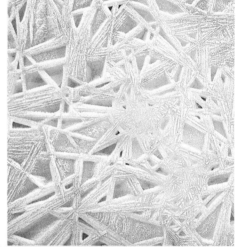

Figure 1–19 *The temperature at which a liquid changes to a solid is called its freezing point. At what temperature does liquid water change to ice crystals?*

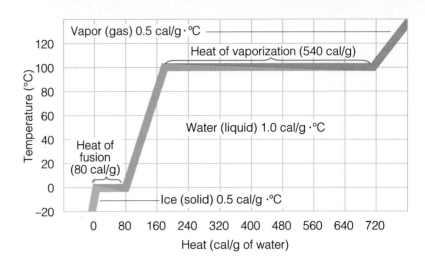

Figure 1–20 *A heating curve, or phase-change diagram, illustrates the fact that during a phase change the addition of heat produces no change in temperature. According to the graph, how many calories per gram are required for ice to melt? For water to vaporize?*

ACTIVITY

/////// THINKING ///////

Mystery Substance

Substance X has a mass of 100 grams. Adding 500 calories of heat causes the temperature of Substance X to rise 10°C. Adding an additional 4000 calories causes half of Substance X to change phase. If enough heat is added to complete the phase change, an additional 1000 calories will be needed to raise the temperature by 10°C. What is Substance X? What is its temperature?

temperature at which a substance changes from the liquid phase to the gas phase is called its **boiling point.** The boiling point of water is 100°C.

During a phase change, something unusual happens. Although there is a change in heat energy (heat is either added or removed), there is no change in temperature. The forces of attraction between molecules are overcome, but the average kinetic energy of the molecules remains the same. Once the melting point or boiling point of a substance has been reached, adding or removing heat results in more of the substance changing phase, not in a change in temperature. Only after a phase change is complete will a change in heat energy result in a change in temperature.

The graph in Figure 1–20 shows the relationship among heat energy, temperature, and phase for water. This type of graph is called a phase-change diagram or a heating curve. According to the diagram, what happens as ice is heated from –20°C to 0°C? The temperature rises as heat is added. For every degree Celsius that the temperature rises, an amount of heat equal to 0.5 cal/g is required. At 0°C the ice undergoes a phase change—the solid ice melts and becomes liquid water. There is no change in temperature during the phase change. How much heat, in calories per gram, is required for this phase change? What is this amount of heat called?

As heat is added to the liquid water after the phase change, the temperature rises again until it reaches 100°C. At this point, even though heat is still being added, the temperature remains at 100°C while the liquid water changes to a gas (steam). This fact has an important application in your daily life. Remember, the heat of vaporization of water is 540 cal/g. So although boiling water and steam have the same temperature, the steam contains 540 cal/g more heat than the water. This means that you can get a more serious burn from steam at 100°C than from boiling water at 100°C.

Once the phase change is complete, the temperature rises again as heat is added to the steam. How many calories of heat are needed to change 1 gram of ice at 0°C to 1 gram of steam at 100°C?

1–4 Section Review

1. What is necessary for a phase change to occur?
2. What is heat of fusion? What is heat of vaporization?
3. What happens to the temperature of a substance during a phase change? What happens to heat energy?

Critical Thinking—*Making Comparisons*
4. Compare the amount of heat released when 54 grams of water freeze to ice with the amount of heat released when 8 grams of steam condense to water.

DISCOVERING

Changing the Boiling Point

  1. Obtain three clean beakers.

  2. Pour 100 mL of water into each beaker.

  3. Add 10 g of salt to the first beaker and 20 g of salt to the second beaker. Do not add anything to the third beaker. Stir to dissolve the salt in each beaker.

  4. Heat the water in each beaker until it begins to boil. Record the temperature at which the water in each beaker begins to boil.

  What is the boiling point of the water in the first beaker? The second beaker? The third beaker?

  ▪ What effect does adding salt to water have on the boiling point of the water?

  ▪ What is the relationship between the amount of salt added and the boiling point?

1–5 Thermal Expansion

Have you ever wondered why sidewalks have spaces between the squares of concrete? The reason is that concrete expands in hot weather. Without the spaces, the surface of the sidewalk would buckle as it expanded. Spaces are left in bridge roadways and between railroad tracks for the same reason.

Have you ever seen a hot-air balloon? As the air inside the balloon is heated, its volume increases and the balloon expands. When the volume of air increases, its density decreases. This is why a hot-air balloon rises.

Guide for Reading

Focus on this question as you read.

▶ *What is meant by thermal expansion?*

Activity
WRITING

Meaningful Relationships

Sometimes words that have a scientific meaning also have another, more common meaning. Often the two meanings are related. Knowing this relationship can help you remember the scientific meaning.

Look up the meaning of each underlined word in the following terms. Then write a sentence that tells how each word's general meaning relates to its scientific meaning.

absolute zero
kinetic energy
potential energy
specific heat
thermal expansion

And you might have noticed that the tires on your bicycle tend to look "higher" in warm weather than they do in cold weather. All of these examples illustrate the process of **thermal expansion.** Thermal expansion is the expansion, or increase in size, of a substance caused by heat. **Most substances—solids, liquids, and gases—expand when their temperature is increased.**

Expansion in Solids

Why do solids expand when they are heated? Knowing something about how molecules are arranged in a solid will help you to answer this question. The molecules of a solid are arranged in fixed positions about which they vibrate, or move in place. As heat energy is added to the solid, the kinetic energy of the molecules increases and their vibrations speed up. The molecules move farther away from their fixed positions and farther away from each other. The increased distance between the molecules accounts for the expansion of the solid.

Expansion in Liquids

The kinetic energy of the molecules in a liquid also increases when the liquid is heated. As the molecules begin to move faster, they move farther apart. So most liquids expand when they are heated.

Figure 1–21 *Thermal expansion is the expansion of a substance due to heat. Solids expand when heated, so expansion links are provided in bridge surfaces. When the temperature is low, the gap between the metal links is large. What happens when the temperature rises?*

Figure 1–22 *Unlike other liquids on Earth, water expands when it freezes. This fact explains why ice floats, an important consideration when ice fishing. How does this fact contribute to potholes on concrete roadways?*

There are exceptions to this rule, however. Between the temperatures of 4°C and 0°C, water expands as it cools. Because of this expansion, the volume of water increases as it cools from 4°C to 0°C. (Volume is the amount of space a substance takes up.) As the volume increases, the density decreases. Density is an important property of matter. The density of a substance is equal to the mass of the substance divided by its volume (Density = Mass/Volume). This equation shows why the density of water changes when its volume changes.

Recall that 0°C is the freezing point of water. So solid ice is less dense than liquid water. You can see this for yourself when you look at ice cubes floating in a glass of water or chunks of ice floating on the surface of a pond. What do you think would be the effect on living things if ice were more dense than liquid water?

ACTIVITY

DOING

A Model Pothole

1. Fill a balloon with water and tie the end securely.

2. In a bowl, mix together equal amounts of flour and salt. Add enough water to the mixture to make a paste.

3. Spread a thick layer of paste over the surface of the balloon. Let the paste dry.

4. Leave the balloon in the freezer compartment of a refrigerator overnight.

What happened to the balloon? What caused this to happen?

You may have noticed "potholes" in roads, especially in the early spring. Potholes are caused when water under the road surface freezes and expands during the winter. The colder the winter, the more potholes in the spring! The expansion of water as it freezes should also remind you not to fill an ice tray to the top with water before putting it in the freezer. Why?

Expansion in Gases

Gas molecules are already farther apart and moving faster than molecules in a solid or a liquid. As the temperature of a gas increases, the molecules move faster and faster. They begin to collide with one another and with the sides of their container. Because the molecules in a gas have considerable freedom of motion, thermal expansion in a gas can be quite dramatic. An explosion may result when a tightly closed container of a gas becomes too hot. Why should you never heat food or anything else in a closed container?

Applications of Thermal Expansion

You are already familiar with one application of thermal expansion—the expansion of a liquid in a thermometer tube as it is heated. The principle of thermal expansion can also be useful in constructing heat-regulating devices. These devices make use of the fact that different solids expand at different rates.

A device that is used to control temperature is called a **thermostat** (THER-muh-stat). Thermostats are used to control the air temperature in homes, schools, and other indoor areas. They are also useful in adjusting the temperature of electric appliances. The switch in a thermostat is a **bimetallic strip,** which consists of two different metals joined together. The two metals have different rates of thermal expansion. When the bimetallic strip is heated, one of the metals expands faster than the other, causing the strip to bend. The metal that expands faster is on the outside of the bimetallic strip. As the temperature changes, the bending and unbending of the bimetallic strip opens and closes an electric circuit

ACTIVITY

DISCOVERING

Thermal Expansion

1. Obtain a metal ball and ring. Pass the ball through the ring.

2. Heat the ball in a candle flame. **CAUTION:** *Be careful when using an open flame.* Pass the heated ball through the ring again.

3. Keep heating the ball and trying to pass it through the ring. Then heat the ring and see if the ball will pass through. Record your observations.

■ Based on your observations, what can you conclude about how solids behave when they are heated?

that controls the heat-regulating device. Thermostats are used on air conditioners, electric blankets, refrigerators, and home heating systems. What are some other uses of thermostats?

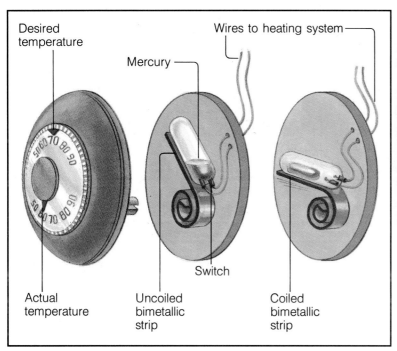

Figure 1–23 *Because the two heated metals in a bimetallic strip expand at different rates, the strip bends. A bimetallic strip is an important part of a thermostat. When the temperature gets too low, the bimetallic strip uncoils. This action causes a drop of mercury to close a switch and start the heating system. What happens when the room temperature then reaches the desired level?*

1–5 Section Review

1. What is meant by thermal expansion?
2. What happens to the molecules of a substance when the substance is heated?
3. How does a bimetallic strip in a thermostat make use of the principle of thermal expansion? What are some uses of thermostats?

Critical Thinking—*Applying Concepts*
4. Use the concept of density to explain why icebergs float in water.

Laboratory Investigation

Finding the Temperature of a Mixture

Problem

When hot and cold water are mixed together, what will be the temperature of the mixture?

Materials *(per group)*

3 Styrofoam cups	ice cubes
2 100-mL graduated cylinders	2 250-mL beakers stirring rod
thermometer	hot plate

Procedure 🧪 👉 ⚡

1. Place several ice cubes in a beaker and fill the beaker about two thirds full with water. Cool the water until the temperature is 10°C or lower.

2. Fill a second beaker about two thirds full with water and heat the beaker until the temperature is at least 75°C. **Note:** *Do not boil the water.*

3. Line up three Styrofoam cups. Pour 40 mL of cold water into the first cup. **Note:** *Be sure that there is no ice in the water.* Pour 40 mL of hot water into the second cup.

4. Measure and record the temperature of the water in each cup.

5. Pour the samples of hot and cold water into the third cup and stir to mix. Measure and record the temperature of the mixture.

6. Discard the water and save the cups for the next steps.

7. Repeat steps 3 through 6 using 80 mL of hot water and 40 mL of cold water.

8. Repeat steps 3 through 6 using 40 mL of hot water and 80 mL of cold water.

9. For each trial, record your observations in a data table.

Observations

For each trial, was the temperature of the mixture closer to the temperature of the hotter sample or of the colder sample? How much closer?

Analysis and Conclusions

1. Explain your observations in each trial.

2. When hot and cold water are mixed, what is one factor that determines the temperature of the mixture?

3. What types of heat transfer are involved when you mix hot and cold water?

4. What are some sources of error in this experiment?

5. **On Your Own** What would you predict the approximate temperature of the mixture to be if you mixed 20 mL of water at 10°C with 100 mL of water at 80°C? Carry out the experiment to test your prediction.

	Cold Water		Hot Water		Mixture	
Trial	*Volume*	*Temperature*	*Volume*	*Temperature*	*Volume*	*Temperature*
1						
2						

Study Guide

Summarizing Key Concepts

1–1 Heat: A Form of Energy

▲ Heat is a form of energy related to the motion of molecules.

▲ The three types of heat transfer are conduction, convection, and radiation.

▲ Substances that conduct heat effectively are called conductors. Substances that do not conduct heat easily are called insulators.

1–2 Temperature and Heat

▲ Kinetic energy is energy of motion.

▲ Temperature is the measure of the average kinetic energy of molecules.The unit used to measure temperature is the degree Celsius.

1–3 Measuring Heat

▲ Heat can be measured indirectly by measuring changes in temperature.

▲ A calorie is the amount of heat needed to raise the temperature of 1 gram of liquid water 1 degree Celsius.

▲ The ability of a substance to absorb heat energy is called its specific heat.

▲ Heat gained or lost by a substance is equal to its mass times the change in temperature times its specific heat.

1–4 Heat and Phase Changes

▲ A phase change involves a gain or loss of heat energy but no change in temperature.

▲ The amount of heat needed to change a substance from the solid phase to the liquid phase is called heat of fusion.

▲ The amount of heat needed to change a substance from the liquid phase to the gas phase is called heat of vaporization.

1–5 Thermal Expansion

▲ Thermal expansion, or the expansion of a substance due to heat, can be explained in terms of the kinetic energy of molecules.

Reviewing Key Terms

Define each term in a complete sentence.

1–1 Heat: A Form of Energy
heat
molecule
heat transfer
conduction
conductor
insulator
convection
radiation

1–2 Temperature and Heat
kinetic energy
temperature
thermometer
Celsius scale
Kelvin scale
absolute zero

1–3 Measuring Heat
calorie
specific heat
calorimeter
potential energy

1–4 Heat and Phase Changes
phase change
heat of fusion
heat of vaporization
freezing point
melting point
boiling point

1–5 Thermal Expansion
thermal expansion
thermostat
bimetallic strip

Chapter Review

Content Review

Multiple Choice

Choose the letter of the answer that best completes each statement.

1. The tube of a thermometer is usually filled with a(an)
   - a. solid.
   - b. liquid.
   - c. gas.
   - d. insulator.
2. When a substance is heated, its molecules
   - a. move faster and farther apart.
   - b. move slower and closer together.
   - c. stay in the same place.
   - d. become larger.
3. Heat is measured in units called
   - a. degrees Celsius.
   - b. kelvins.
   - c. calories.
   - d. specific heat units.
4. The freezing point of a substance is the same as its
   - a. boiling point.
   - b. evaporation point.
   - c. melting point.
   - d. condensation point.

5. All of the following materials are good conductors of heat except
   - a. copper.
   - b. silver.
   - c. wood.
   - d. aluminum.
6. The energy that is stored in fuels and foods is called
   - a. kinetic energy.
   - b. food energy.
   - c. caloric energy.
   - d. potential energy.
7. The phase change that takes place when a gas becomes a liquid is called
   - a. evaporation.
   - b. condensation.
   - c. boiling.
   - d. freezing.
8. A temperature of $20°C$ is equal to
   - a. 293 K.
   - b. 253 K.
   - c. –253 K.
   - d. –293 K.

True or False

If the statement is true, write "true." If it is false, change the underlined word or words to make the statement true.

1. Heat is transferred through liquids and gases by <u>radiation</u>.
2. Fast-moving molecules have <u>less</u> heat energy than slow-moving molecules.
3. An instrument used to measure temperature is a <u>calorimeter</u>.
4. Heat can be measured in calories or <u>kelvins</u>.
5. During a phase change, the temperature <u>does not</u> change.
6. Solid ice is <u>more</u> dense than liquid water.
7. Absolute zero is equal to the lowest reading on the <u>Kelvin</u> temperature scale.

Concept Mapping

Complete the following concept map for Section 1–1. Refer to pages Q6–Q7 to construct a concept map for the entire chapter.

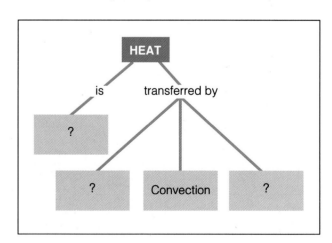

Concept Mastery

Discuss each of the following in a brief paragraph.

1. How did Count Rumford's experiment challenge the caloric theory of heat?
2. Explain why a temperature of –273°C is called absolute zero.
3. What is the relationship among work, heat, and energy?
4. Compare temperature and heat.
5. How does a thermometer make use of the property of thermal expansion?
6. Describe how a thermostat controls the temperature in a house.
7. Why does an ice cube float in water instead of sinking to the bottom of the glass?

Critical Thinking and Problem Solving

Use the skills you have developed in this chapter to answer each of the following.

1. **Applying concepts** Why is the air pressure in a car's tires different before and after the car has been driven for several hours?
2. **Interpreting graphs** Using the heating curve in Figure 1–20, explain what would happen to a 5-gram ice cube at 0°C if it were to gain 1000 calories of heat.
3. **Interpreting diagrams**
   a. In which container(s) is the heat content greatest?
   b. In which containers is the motion of molecules the same?
   c. Compare the motion of molecules in containers A and C.
   d. Compare the average kinetic energy of containers A and B.
   e. Which container needs the greatest number of calories to raise the temperature by 1 Celsius degree?
4. **Making comparisons** Compare the three methods of heat transfer in terms of how heat moves and the types of substances in which the transfer takes place.
5. **Applying concepts** Refer to the drawing of a thermos bottle in Figure 1–7 on page17. Explain the importance of the cap, vacuum, double-walled glass bottle, and air space in preventing heat transfer.
6. **Analyzing data** A chemical reaction takes place in a calorimeter. The following data are obtained:

mass of water	500 g
initial temperature of water	30°C
final temperature of water	45°C

   How much heat, in calories and kilocalories, is released in this reaction?
7. **Using the writing process** Haiku is a form of poetry that began in Japan. A haiku has three lines. The first and third lines have five syllables each. The second line has seven syllables. Haiku may be used to describe scenes in nature and to express feelings. Write a haiku describing how you might feel on a frosty winter day or a sweltering summer day.

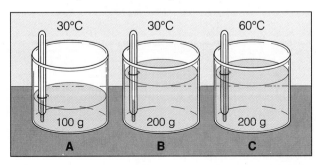

30°C	30°C	60°C
100 g	200 g	200 g
A	B	C

Uses of Heat

Guide for Reading

After you read the following sections, you will be able to

2–1 Heating Systems
- ■ Distinguish among various types of heating systems.

2–2 Insulation
- ■ Explain how insulation prevents heat loss.

2–3 Cooling Systems
- ■ Describe the operation of a cooling system.

2–4 Heat Engines
- ■ Explain how heat engines convert heat energy into mechanical energy.

2–5 Thermal Pollution
- ■ Define thermal pollution and discuss its effects on the environment.

The year is 2064. Across the Midwest, an area at one time called the breadbasket of the nation, desert sands cover the once-fertile fields. In Arizona, the former desert is covered with the green, leafy canopy of a rain forest. Much of the coastline of eastern New York, including the skyscrapers of Manhattan, is under water.

Does this sound like a science fiction story? Although you may think these scenes are unbelievable, they are within the realm of possibility. Scientists report that the temperature of the Earth is gradually rising due to the greenhouse effect. Like the glass in a greenhouse, carbon dioxide and other gases in the Earth's atmosphere trap infrared radiation (heat) from the sun. The result is a kind of "heat blanket" wrapped around the Earth.

If the greenhouse effect continues to raise the Earth's temperature, heat may dramatically affect your life in the future. But did you know that heat plays an important role in your daily life right now? In this chapter you will learn how heat is obtained, used, and controlled. The more we understand about heat today, the better our chances may be of avoiding the greenhouse effect in the future.

Journal *Activity*

You and Your World In your journal, describe what you think your life might be like 20 or 30 years from now if the greenhouse effect continues to cause an increase in the Earth's temperature.

An artist's conception of what Manhattan may look like in the future if the greenhouse effect continues to raise Earth's average temperature

2–1 Heating Systems

Controlling the temperature of an indoor environment is one way to use an understanding of heat for a practical application. If you have ever been in a building that was either too hot or too cold, you know the importance of a good heating system. Most office buildings, homes, and apartment houses in the United States have **central heating systems** that provide comfortable environments for daily activities. **A central heating system generates heat for an entire building or group of buildings from one central location.** After the heat is generated, it is delivered where it is needed.

Based on how the heat is delivered, central heating systems are divided into two main groups: direct systems and indirect systems. A direct system circulates warm air throughout the area to be heated. An indirect system circulates hot water or steam through

Figure 2–1 *Heating systems have certainly changed over the years as people have progressed from fires in caves to warm hearths in a country home to a modern building heated entirely by the heat given off by computers.*

pipes that lead to convectors or radiators. The convectors or radiators then give off heat in the area to be heated. Look around your home or classroom as you read this section. Can you tell what kind of heating system is in use? How do you know?

Although there are different types of central heating systems, they all require a source of heat, such as electricity or the burning of a fuel. All central heating systems also have automatic controls. These controls regulate the temperature of the area being heated, turn off the system if any part of it becomes dangerously overheated, and prevent the system from starting if conditions are unsafe.

Hot-Water Heating

A **hot-water system** consists of a network of pipes and convectors connected to a hot-water heater. Fuel burned in the hot-water heater raises the temperature of the water to about 82°C. (Remember, the boiling point of water is 100°C.) Then the water is pumped through pipes to a convector in each room. The hot water heats the convector. The heat given off by the convector is circulated throughout the room by convection currents. After the water has lost some of its heat, it returns to the hot-water heater through another pipe.

Figure 2–2 *A hot-water heating system (left) and a steam-heating system (right) are two common central heating systems that are quite similar. What is the major difference between the two systems?*

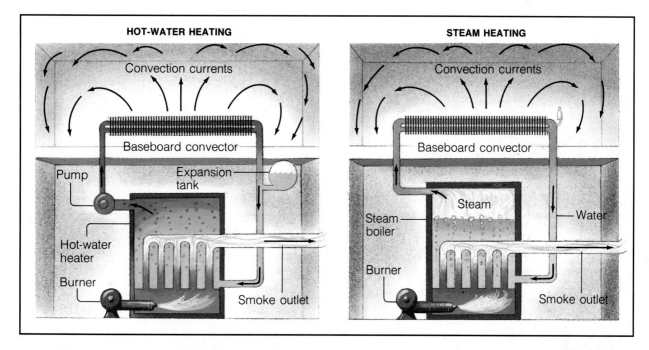

Steam Heating

A **steam-heating system** is similar to a hot-water system except that the water is changed into steam in a boiler. The steam is then forced through pipes to the convectors, where it gives off heat to the room. In giving off heat, the steam condenses, or changes from the gas phase to the liquid phase. The condensed steam, or water, then flows back to the boiler, where it is heated and changed into steam again.

Radiant Hot-Water Heating

In a **radiant hot-water system,** water is heated in a hot-water heater and then transferred to a continuous coil of pipe in the floor of each room. As heat radiates from the pipe, a nearly uniform temperature is maintained from floor to ceiling. This means that the temperature difference between the floor and the ceiling is only a few degrees. Why do you think radiant hot-water heating provides a more even temperature than steam heating or hot-water heating?

Figure 2–3 *In these central heating systems, heat is transferred by radiation. The source of heat in a radiant hot-water system (left) is hot water. In a radiant electric system (right), the source of heat is electricity.*

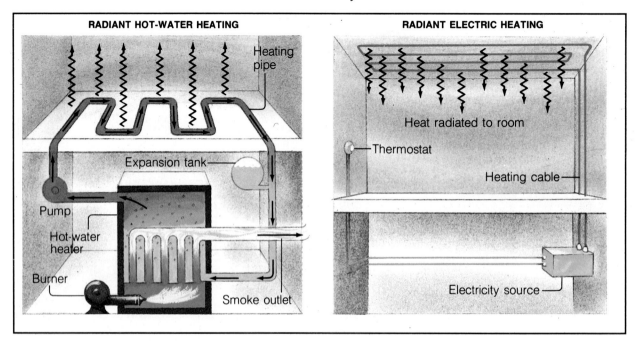

Radiant Electric Heating

The source of heat for a **radiant electric system** is electricity. As electricity passes through wires or cables, the wires or cables resist the flow of electricity. As a result of this resistance, heat is produced. Think of the coils of wire in a toaster. As electricity passes through the wire, the heat produced toasts your bread or muffin.

The wires or cables in a radiant electric system can be installed in the ceiling, floor, baseboards, or walls of a room. The heat produced is radiated to all parts of the room. A thermostat, which is often installed in each room or local area, controls the amount of heat produced by the wires or cables.

Warm-Air Heating

A **warm-air system** consists of a furnace, a blower, pipelike connections called ducts, and vents that open into each room to be heated. The furnace heats the air, which is then forced by the blower through the ducts to the vents. Convection currents keep the warm air moving as it transfers its heat to the surrounding air. Cool air returns to the furnace by a separate duct. As the air circulates, filters remove dust particles.

Figure 2–4 *In a warm-air system (left), hot air from a furnace is forced to vents through pipelike connections called ducts. How is heat transferred in this system? A heat-pump system (right) takes heat from the outside and brings it inside—even in cold weather! What two phase changes are involved in this heating system?*

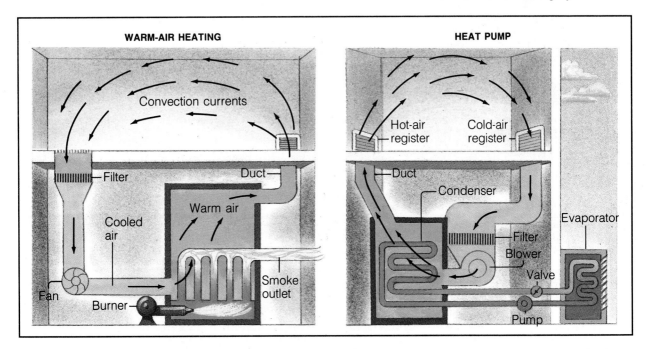

WARM-AIR HEATING

Convection currents

Filter

Duct

Warm air

Cooled air

Fan

Burner

Smoke outlet

HEAT PUMP

Hot-air register

Cold-air register

Duct

Condenser

Evaporator

Filter

Blower

Valve

Pump

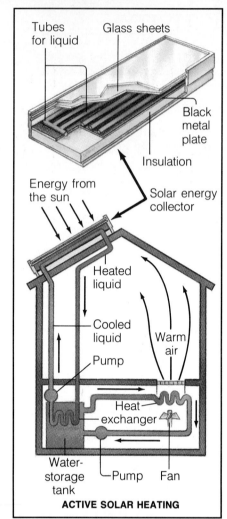

Tubes for liquid
Glass sheets
Black metal plate
Insulation
Energy from the sun
Solar energy collector
Heated liquid
Cooled liquid
Warm air
Pump
Heat exchanger
Water-storage tank
Pump
Fan

ACTIVE SOLAR HEATING

Figure 2–5 *Water in the solar panel of an active solar system is heated by the sun and piped to a storage tank. Here it heats water in the water tank. This heated water then circulates through pipes to heat the house. Why is the metal plate in the solar panel painted black?*

Heat Pumps

A **heat-pump system** is based on the principle that the Earth or outside air contains heat energy that can be used to heat an indoor area—even in cold weather! What a heat pump actually does is take heat from outside a building and bring it inside.

Through a coil outside the building that is to be heated, a heat pump circulates a liquid that evaporates (changes from the liquid phase to the gas phase) at a low temperature. As the liquid passes through the coil, it picks up heat from the air or the ground. Eventually the liquid gains enough heat to change to a gas. The gas travels into a compressor, where an increase in pressure results in an increase in temperature. The hot gas then passes to a coil inside the building, where it heats the air. The warm air is forced through ducts and circulated through each room just as in a warm-air system.

Once the hot gas has given off its heat, it condenses into a hot liquid. The hot liquid is then cooled as it passes through a pressure-reducing valve. Finally, the cooled liquid is pumped into the outdoor coil to begin the process all over again. What might be some disadvantages in this type of heating system?

Solar Heating

A **solar-heating system** uses the energy of the sun to produce heat. There are two basic types of solar-heating systems: active solar heating and passive solar heating.

An **active solar-heating system** includes a device for collecting solar energy (called a solar collector), a place to store the heat, and a means for circulating the heat throughout a building. The diagram in Figure 2–5 shows a typical active solar-heating system. Refer to the diagram as you read the description that follows.

The solar collector, also called a flat-plate collector, consists of a metal plate painted black on the side that faces the sun. (Black absorbs sunlight better than any other color.) As the sunlight is absorbed, the plate heats up. On the surface of

Activity Bank

Let the Sun Shine In, p.78

Figure 2–6 *In the Mojave Desert, California, hundreds of mirrors in an array called Solar One reflect solar radiation onto a tower filled with water. How might the heated water in the tower be used?*

the plate is an array of metal tubing. Water, or some other liquid, circulates through the tubing. The tubing is covered by glass or clear plastic to keep it from losing heat. Why do you think glass or clear plastic is used for this purpose?

As sunlight strikes the collector, heat is absorbed. The heat absorbed by the collector is transferred to the water. The heated water flows through a tube into a storage tank. Here the heat from the water in the tube is transferred to the water in the tank by a heat exchanger in the tank. The hot water circulates through pipes to heat the building or to heat air blown into the building. In the meantime, a pump returns the cool water to the collector to be reheated by the sun. On cloudy days, when the solar collector cannot absorb enough solar energy to produce hot water and the storage system has cooled, a backup heating system is used.

In a **passive solar-heating system,** a building is heated directly by the rays of the sun. To get the most heat from a passive solar system, the building must be designed with the placement, size, and orientation of the windows in mind.

ACTIVITY

DISCOVERING

Black and White

Try this activity to demonstrate the effect of color on heat. You will need a piece of black construction paper, a piece of white construction paper, a candle, and an electric light bulb.

1. Light the candle. **CAUTION:** *Be careful when using an open flame.* Let one drop of wax from the candle fall on each piece of construction paper. Blow out the candle.

2. Hold both pieces of construction paper exactly the same distance from an electric light bulb. On which piece of paper does the wax melt first?

■ If you want to keep cool on a hot summer day, should you wear dark-colored clothes or light-colored clothes? Why?

Heat From the Sun

1. Place a piece of paper on a flat surface in direct sunlight.

2. Hold a small magnifying glass (such as a hand lens) above the paper.

3. Position the magnifying glass so that the sun's rays are focused to a point on the paper. What happens to the paper? Why?

Because of the variations in the amount of solar energy received at a particular location, passive solar systems are usually not the only source of heat for a building. A backup heating system usually must be used with a passive solar system. The backup system provides heat when sunlight is not available or when the heat collected during the day is not enough to keep the building warm on a cold night. What conditions do you think affect the amount of solar energy a location receives?

Figure 2–7 *To keep itself warm on cold days, this iguana basks in the sun. Is the iguana using a form of active or passive solar heating?*

2–1 Section Review

1. What is a central heating system?
2. How does a steam-heating system differ from a hot-water system?
3. Describe how a radiant electric system produces heat. Why is this system different from other central heating systems?
4. What is the basic difference between an active solar-heating system and a passive solar-heating system?

Critical Thinking—*Sequencing Events*
5. Describe in order the heat transfers and phase changes involved in a heat-pump system.

2-2 Insulation

What happens after a central heating system brings heat into a building? Once heat is brought into a room or building, it will quickly begin to escape if the area does not have proper **insulation.** Recall from Chapter 1 that insulating materials reduce heat transfer because they are poor conductors of heat. **Insulation prevents heat loss by reducing the transfer of heat that occurs by conduction and convection.**

A common insulating material is **fiberglass.** Fiberglass consists of long, thin strands of glass packed together. In between the strands of glass are air spaces. Glass is a poor conductor of heat. So is the air that is trapped between the glass fibers. A down-filled vest or jacket uses the same principle to keep you warm in winter. Air trapped in the spaces between the down prevents the loss of body heat. (Down is the inner layer of soft, fluffy feathers on birds such as ducks and geese. How do you think down feathers help keep birds warm?)

Insulating materials are packed beneath roofs and in the outside walls of buildings. Insulation can also be used around doors and windows. This type

Guide for Reading

Focus on these questions as you read.

▶ *What is insulation?*
▶ *How does insulation prevent heat loss?*

Activity Bank

Turn Down the Heat, p.79

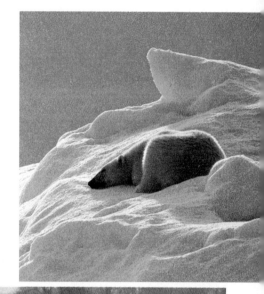

Figure 2–8 *How does insulation protect the polar bear, the bison, and the geese from the cold?*

Figure 2–9 *Invisible heat energy, or infrared energy, can be "seen" by using a device called a thermograph. This thermogram, or heat picture, reveals heat loss from a house. Generally, the lighter and brighter the color, the greater the heat loss. How can a thermogram be useful to homeowners?*

ACTIVITY

of insulation is called weatherstripping. Weatherstripping prevents heat loss by closing off spaces through which heat can be transferred by convection. Double-pane window glass is another effective insulator. The air trapped between the panes of glass does not conduct heat well. In addition, the air space is so small that heat transfer by convection cannot take place.

A well-insulated building is as comfortable in hot weather as it is in cold weather. In cold weather, insulation keeps heat inside the building. In hot weather, the insulation keeps heat out. The building is kept relatively cool as heat from the outside is prevented from entering the building by either conduction or convection. Good insulation also helps lower fuel costs. Why do you think this is so?

2–2 Section Review

1. What is insulation? What is the purpose of insulation?
2. How does fiberglass prevent heat loss?
3. Why is good insulation important in both hot weather and cold weather?
4. Explain how insulation prevents heat loss by both conduction and convection.

Connection—*You and Your World*
5. The cardboard used to make pizza boxes is naturally brown in color. Why would the companies that manufacture the boxes spend extra money to make them white? What else could they do to the boxes to make them better insulators?

Figure 2–10 *Believe it or not, blocks of ice can be used to insulate a home, as this Eskimo of the Arctic Circle well knows. How is an igloo insulated?*

2–3 Cooling Systems

Guide for Reading

Focus on this question as you read.

▶ *How does a cooling system work?*

Have you ever had this experience? On a hot summer day, you jump into a swimming pool to cool off. After climbing out of the swimming pool, you feel a chill—even though the sun is just as hot as it was before you got wet. What causes this cooling effect? The cooling effect is due to evaporation. The water molecules on your skin absorb heat from your body as the water evaporates, or changes from the liquid phase to the gas phase. This absorption of heat lowers your body temperature. Thus evaporation is a cooling process.

You can test the cooling effect of evaporation for yourself. Put a drop of water on the back of your hand. Now blow gently on your hand. Which feels cooler: the wet skin or the dry skin? How does perspiration help cool you when you are overheated? **The process of evaporation is used by cooling systems to remove heat energy from a room, building, or other enclosed space.** Refrigerators, air conditioners, and dehumidifiers all contain **cooling systems.**

A cooling system consists of four basic parts: a storage tank, a freezer unit, a compressor, and condenser coils. A cooling system also contains a refrigerant. The refrigerant is the liquid that is evaporated. Refrigerants evaporate at a low temperature. Many cooling systems use Freon (FREE-ahn) as the refrigerant. Another common refrigerant is ammonia.

The diagram in Figure 2–11 shows how a typical refrigerator system works. Liquid Freon in the storage tank is pumped to the freezer unit. As the liquid refrigerant evaporates, it absorbs heat from the freezer compartment. So the inside of the refrigerator becomes cool. The Freon gas then flows to a compressor, where the pressure of the gas (and its temperature) is increased. The hot gaseous Freon then passes through the condenser coils, where it loses its heat and changes back into a liquid. The liquid Freon then returns to the storage tank and the process begins again.

The heat removed from the freezer compartment of a refrigerator is radiated from the condenser coils to the outside air. The condenser coils are often

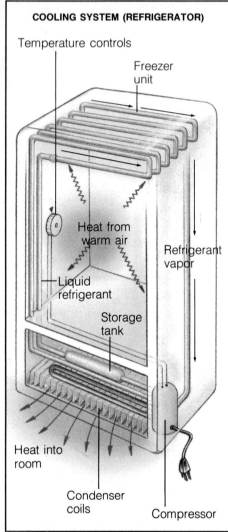

COOLING SYSTEM (REFRIGERATOR)

Temperature controls

Freezer unit

Heat from warm air

Liquid refrigerant

Refrigerant vapor

Storage tank

Heat into room

Condenser coils

Compressor

Figure 2–11 *Without refrigeration systems, ice hockey could not be an indoor sport. In this diagram, you can see how the basic parts of a refrigerator work as a cooling system. What phase change takes place in the freezer unit? In the condenser coils?*

PROBLEM Solving

Freon and the Ozone Layer

High in the Earth's atmosphere is a layer of gas called the ozone layer. Ozone is a form of oxygen. The ozone layer blocks harmful ultraviolet radiation from the sun from reaching the Earth. (Ultraviolet radiation can cause certain types of skin cancer.) The Freon used in refrigerators eventually escapes into the atmosphere and reaches the ozone layer, where it changes some of the ozone into oxygen. Not too long ago, scientists discovered a "hole" in the ozone layer over Antarctica.

This satellite map shows severe holes (blue areas) in the ozone layer over Antarctica.

Relating Cause and Effect

1. What might happen to the ozone layer if more and more Freon is produced and released into the atmosphere?
2. What effect might this have on human health?
3. What do you think might be done in the future to help protect the ozone layer?

---

located on the back of a refrigerator. Fans are sometimes used to blow away the air that is heated by the coils. You should be careful not to touch the coils, which can become quite hot. Although you may think it sounds strange, you can burn yourself on a refrigerator!

2–3 Section Review

1. How does a cooling system use the process of evaporation?
2. What are the basic parts of a cooling system?
3. What is a refrigerant? What happens to the refrigerant in a cooling system?

Connection—*You and Your World*

4. Is it a good idea to try to cool a room by opening the door of the refrigerator? Why or why not?

ACTIVITY DOING

Evaporation and Cooling

1. Place a drop of water on the back of your hand. How does your hand feel as the water evaporates?
2. Repeat step 1 using a drop of rubbing alcohol. Is there any difference in the rate of evaporation?
3. Wrap a small piece of wet cotton around the bulb of a thermometer. Fan it gently with a piece of cardboard. What happens to the temperature?

2-4 Heat Engines

You learned in Chapter 1 that the experiments of Rumford and Joule showed that work produces heat. **Heat engines** make use of the reverse process. **Heat engines are machines that convert heat energy into mechanical energy in order to do work.** (Any form of energy, such as heat, can be converted into any other form of energy.) Mechanical energy is the energy associated with motion. What is another name for energy of motion?

All heat engines involve **combustion.** Combustion is the burning of a fuel. During combustion, a fuel is heated to a temperature at which it combines with oxygen in the air and gives off heat. Heat engines are classified into two main types according to where combustion takes place.

External-Combustion Engines

In an **external-combustion engine,** fuel is burned outside the engine. The steam engine is an example of an external-combustion engine. In a steam engine, steam is heated in a boiler outside the engine and then passed through a valve into the engine. In early steam engines, the steam pushed

Figure 2–12 *An external-combustion engine, as shown in the diagram, converts heat energy into mechanical energy. The wheels of a steam train are powered by an external-combustion engine.*

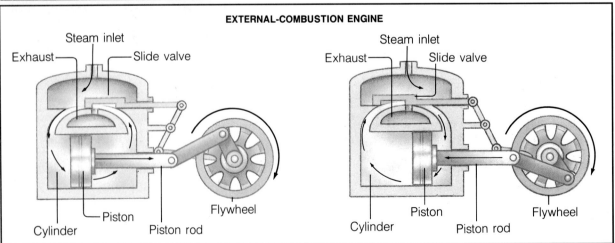

EXTERNAL-COMBUSTION ENGINE

Exhaust — Steam inlet — Slide valve
Cylinder — Piston — Piston rod — Flywheel

Exhaust — Steam inlet — Slide valve
Cylinder — Piston — Piston rod — Flywheel

against a metal plate called a piston, which moved back and forth in a tube called a cylinder. The movement of the piston transferred mechanical energy to a connecting rod, which then did some kind of work, such as turning the wheels of a train or the propellers of a steamship.

Modern steam engines do not use a piston and a cylinder. Instead, steam under great pressure is passed through holes onto paddle wheels called turbines. The turbines, which rotate like high-speed windmills, produce mechanical energy. A steam turbine is more efficient than a piston and a cylinder because it wastes less energy.

Internal-Combustion Engine

When the burning of a fuel takes place inside an engine, the engine is called an **internal-combustion engine.** A familiar type of internal-combustion engine is the gasoline engine, which powers most cars.

Most gasoline engines are four-stroke engines. The diagram in Figure 2–13 on page 56 shows the four strokes that make up each cycle in a gasoline engine. In the first stroke, the piston inside the cylinder moves down and the intake valve opens. Gasoline that was changed from a liquid to a gas and mixed with air in the carburetor (KAHR-buh-rayt-er) enters the cylinder through the intake valve. This process is the intake stroke.

The intake valve closes and the piston moves to the top of the cylinder. As it does, the gaseous mixture is compressed, or squeezed together, so that the volume of the mixture is greatly reduced. This process is the compression stroke.

At this point in the four-stroke cycle, with both valves closed, a spark plug produces an electric spark that ignites the compressed fuel mixture. The explosion of hot gases increases the volume of the mixture and forces the piston back down in the cylinder. This is the power stroke. At this point energy is transferred from the piston to the wheels of the car by a series of shafts and gears.

In the final stroke, the exhaust valve opens. The piston moves to the top of the cylinder and expels gases through the exhaust valve. This process is called the exhaust stroke.

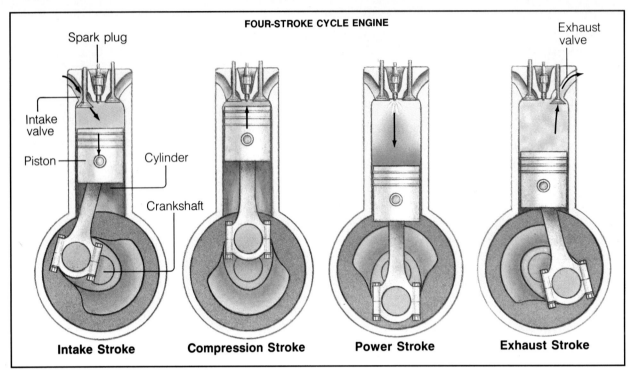

FOUR-STROKE CYCLE ENGINE

Spark plug

Exhaust valve

Intake valve

Piston

Cylinder

Crankshaft

Intake Stroke   **Compression Stroke**   **Power Stroke**   **Exhaust Stroke**

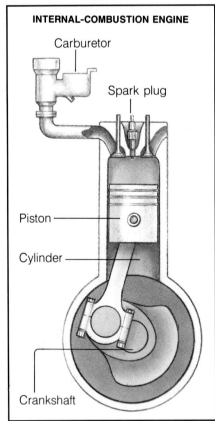

INTERNAL-COMBUSTION ENGINE

Carburetor

Spark plug

Piston

Cylinder

Crankshaft

Figure 2–13 *A gasoline engine is a four-stroke internal-combustion engine. Here you see the processes involved in each stroke. During which stroke is energy transferred from the piston to the wheels of the car?*

As the piston moves back down, more gaseous fuel and air mixture from the carburetor enters the cylinder to begin the four-stroke cycle again. A fixed amount of gasoline is used in each cycle, and waste products are given off as exhaust at the end of each cycle. It is important to use clean-burning fuel in car engines to reduce the amount of impurities given off in the exhaust.

A diesel engine, like a gasoline engine, is an internal-combustion engine. But in a diesel engine, only air is taken in during the intake stroke. At the end of the compression stroke, a measured amount of fuel is injected into the compressed air in the cylinder. The compression of the air raises its temperature high enough so that the fuel ignites at once. For this reason a diesel engine does not need spark plugs. Why do you think a diesel engine might more correctly be called a compression-ignition engine?

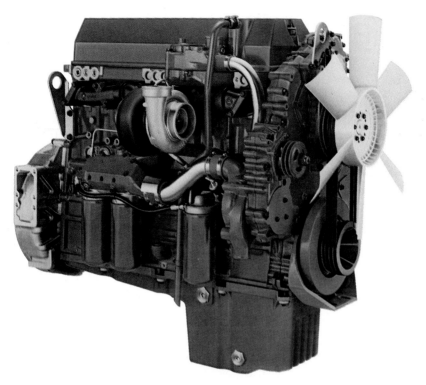

Figure 2–14 *Diesel engines are more efficient than gasoline engines. However, diesel engines have some drawbacks. They may be difficult to start in cold weather and tend to be noisier than gasoline engines.*

2–4 Section Review

1. How does a heat engine work?
2. What are the two main types of heat engines? How are they different?
3. Describe what happens in the four-stroke cycle of a gasoline engine. How is this different from what happens in a diesel engine?

Critical Thinking—*Applying Concepts*

4. Several car manufacturers are working on cars that use two-stroke engines instead of four-stroke engines. These two-stroke engines eliminate the intake stroke and the exhaust stroke, and they make use of modern fuel-injection techniques during the compression stroke. Why do you think a two-stroke engine might be more efficient than a four-stroke engine?

ACTIVITY

READING

Earth's Future?

How could such human activities as thermal pollution, the greenhouse effect, and the thinning of the ozone layer possibly affect the Earth's future? For a look at what the Earth might be like in the year 2038, read the science-fiction novel *Earth* by David Brin.

2–5 Thermal Pollution

Modern technology could not exist without the use of heat energy. Yet like many aspects of technology, heat energy can be harmful to the environment. The environment includes the air, land, and water.

Much of the heat generated by industrial processes and power plants cannot be used. It is waste heat. This waste heat is often released directly into the atmosphere. Or it may be released as hot water—just dumped into nearby rivers and lakes. **Thermal pollution** results. Pollution is anything that damages the environment. **Thermal pollution occurs when waste heat damages the environment by causing an unnatural rise in temperature.**

Thermal pollution endangers the survival of plants and animals. Fishes are especially vulnerable to increases in water temperature. Some species can survive only a few hours at temperatures above 25°C.

What can be done to reduce thermal pollution from factories and power plants? One solution is the use of a cooling tower. In a cooling tower, hot water from a factory or power plant is cooled as it flows through pipes. By the time the water is released into a nearby river or lake, it has cooled enough so that it is no longer a threat to fishes and other wildlife.

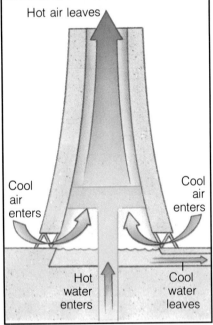

Hot air leaves

Cool air enters

Cool air enters

Hot water enters

Cool water leaves

Figure 2–15 *These cooling towers at a nuclear-power plant are used to reduce thermal pollution. Hot water from the power plant is cooled as it flows through pipes suspended in the tower. Why is thermal pollution harmful?*

2–5 Section Review

1. What is thermal pollution? What types of wildlife are threatened by thermal pollution?
2. What is the source of the heat that causes thermal pollution?
3. According to Figure 2–15 what happens to the excess heat after the water is cooled in the cooling tower?

Connection—*Life Science*

4. Manatees are aquatic mammals that live in warm rivers and streams in Florida. These animals are attracted to the hot water released by power plants. How might the manatees be affected if the power plants were shut down?

CONNECTIONS

Using Cold to Fight Cancer

What does heat—or rather the lack of it—have to do with cancer? Doctors are presently testing a new way to use *cryosurgery* to combat some forms of cancer. The prefix *cryo-* means cold or freezing. Cryosurgery is the use of extreme cold to destroy diseased tissue. This is not a new technique. Dermatologists have used cryosurgery for years to destroy skin tumors. What is new is the way in which cryosurgery can now be used to destroy cancerous tumors inside the body.

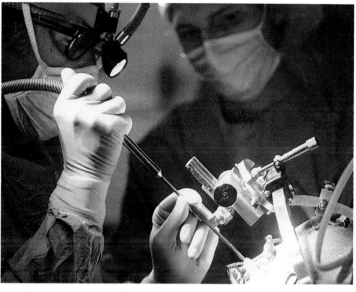

When cancer cells spread through the body, one of the internal organs in which they may settle is the liver. Today, more than 65,000 people in the United States develop liver cancer every year. Conventional surgery for liver cancer is complicated and dangerous (and sometimes impossible). Few liver cancer patients survive more than a few years after surgery.

Cryosurgery involves using a thin probe to freeze tumors. Once the probe has been inserted into the liver, liquid nitrogen at a temperature of about –200°C flows through the probe and freezes the tumor, destroying the cancer cells. Surgeons can watch this process, which takes about 15 minutes, on an ultrasound monitor.

The long-term survival rate for liver cancer patients following cryosurgery has been found to be much higher than for conventional surgery. Doctors are now attempting to refine this technique and to expand its use to destroy tumors in other parts of the body, including the brain.

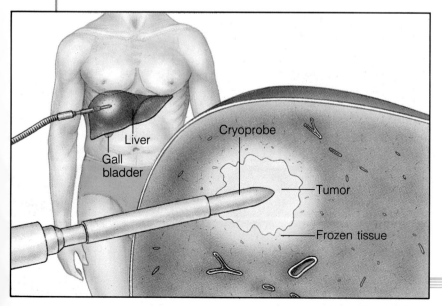

Liver

Gall bladder

Cryoprobe

Tumor

Frozen tissue

Laboratory Investigation

Building a Solar Collector

Problem

How can solar energy be collected?

Materials (per group)

shoe box, painted black on the inside
newspaper, painted black
rubber or plastic tubing, 1 mm diameter x
  1 m long
funnel   container, 1 L capacity
ring stand and ring   graduated cylinder
thermometer   plastic wrap
250-mL beaker   pencil

Procedure 🧪

1. Fill the inside of the shoe box with crumpled newspaper. Using a pencil, punch a hole in each end of the shoe box, as shown in the diagram.
2. Insert the tubing through the holes and position it inside the box as shown. Be sure to leave at least 10 cm of tubing sticking out each end of the box.
3. Cover the box tightly with plastic wrap.
4. Place the box in direct sunlight, tilting one end so that it is about 5 cm higher than the other end.
5. Attach the funnel to the tubing at the higher end of the box. Use the ring stand and ring to hold the funnel in place.
6. Position a beaker at the other end of the box to serve as the collecting beaker.
7. Fill the container with 1 L of water at room temperature. Measure and record the temperature of the water.
8. Pour 200 mL of water from the container into the graduated cylinder.
9. Now pour the 200 mL of water from the graduated cylinder into the funnel.

10. Repeat steps 8 and 9 for a total of five trials. After every trial, record the number of the trial and the temperature of the water in the collecting beaker. **Note:** *Empty the collecting beaker after every trial.*
11. Record your data on a graph. Plot the trial number along the X axis and the water temperature along the Y axis.

Observations

What happened to the water temperature as the number of trials increased? Does your graph support this observation?

Analysis and Conclusions

1. How can you explain the different temperatures that you recorded?
2. **On Your Own** How could you make your solar collector more effective?

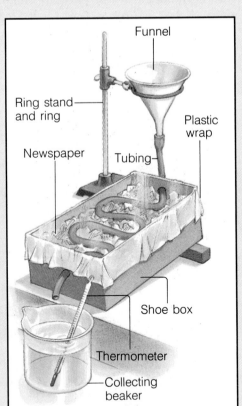

Study Guide

Summarizing Key Concepts

2–1 Heating Systems

▲ Based on the way heat is delivered, central heating systems are classified as direct or indirect systems.

▲ Major types of central heating systems include hot water, steam, radiant hot water, radiant electric, warm air, heat pump, and solar.

2–2 Insulation

▲ Insulation prevents heat loss by reducing the transfer of heat from a building by conduction and convection.

▲ Insulating a building is as important in hot weather as it is in cold weather.

2–3 Cooling Systems

▲ Cooling systems use the process of evaporation to remove heat from the surroundings.

▲ A cooling system consists of a storage tank, freezer unit, compressor, condenser coils, and refrigerant.

▲ A refrigerant is a liquid that evaporates at a low temperature.

2–4 Heat Engines

▲ Heat engines convert heat energy into mechanical energy to do work.

▲ All heat engines involve combustion, or the burning of a fuel.

▲ In an external-combustion engine, fuel is burned outside the engine.

▲ In an internal-combustion engine, such as a gasoline engine, fuel is burned inside the engine.

▲ The four strokes in a gasoline engine are the intake stroke, the compression stroke, the power stroke, and the exhaust stroke.

2–5 Thermal Pollution

▲ Thermal pollution occurs when waste heat damages the environment by causing an unnatural rise in temperature.

Reviewing Key Terms

Define each term in a complete sentence.

2–1 Heating Systems
central heating system
hot-water system
steam-heating system
radiant hot-water system
radiant electric system
warm-air system
heat-pump system
solar-heating system
active solar-heating system
passive solar-heating system

2–2 Insulation
insulation
fiberglass

2–3 Cooling Systems
cooling system

2–4 Heat Engines
heat engine
combustion
external-combustion engine
internal-combustion engine

2–5 Thermal Pollution
thermal pollution

Chapter Review

Content Review

Multiple Choice

Choose the letter of the answer that best completes each statement.

1. The heating system that uses the energy of the sun to produce heat is a
   a. radiant hot-water system.
   b. radiant electric system.
   c. solar-heating system.
   d. warm-air system.
2. Heat engines convert heat energy into
   a. chemical energy.
   b. mechanical energy.
   c. light energy.
   d. nuclear energy.
3. Which of the following is an insulating material?
   a. fiberglass
   c. copper
   b. Freon
   d. ammonia
4. Thermal pollution damages the environment by increasing
   a. dust particles in the air.
   b. engine exhaust.
   c. infrared radiation.
   d. temperature.

5. A cooling system contains all of the following parts except a(an)
   a. compressor.
   c. freezer unit.
   b. storage tank.
   d. exhaust valve.
6. All central heating systems require a(an)
   a. refrigerant.
   c. insulator.
   b. heat source.
   d. compressor.
7. One way to reduce thermal pollution is by using a
   a. turbine.
   c. cooling system.
   b. cooling tower.
   d. heating system.
8. In a cooling system, condenser coils are used to
   a. change the refrigerant from a liquid to a gas.
   b. increase the pressure of the refrigerant.
   c. change the refrigerant from a gas back into a liquid.
   d. increase the temperature of the refrigerant.

True or False

If the statement is true, write "true." If it is false, change the underlined word or words to make the statement true.

1. A solar collector is part of a <u>passive</u> solar-heating system.
2. Double-pane window glass prevents heat loss by reducing heat transfer by convection and <u>radiation</u>.
3. Thermal pollution probably <u>would not</u> be a problem for fishes living in a lake near a power plant.
4. In a diesel engine, fuel is injected into the cylinder during the <u>intake</u> stroke.
5. The type of heating system that produces a nearly uniform temperature in a room is a <u>steam-heating</u> system.

Concept Mapping

Complete the following concept map for Section 2–1. Refer to pages Q6–Q7 to construct a concept map for the entire chapter.

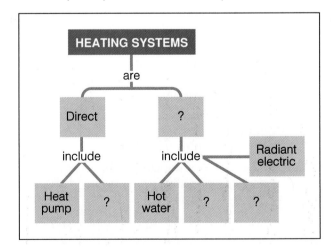

Concept Mastery

Discuss each of the following in a brief paragraph.

1. Assume that a factory or power plant is located near each of the following: an ocean, a river, and a lake. Which body of water would probably be most affected by thermal pollution? Which would be least affected? Explain your answers.
2. Choose one type of heat engine and describe how it changes heat energy into mechanical energy to do work.
3. Choose one type of central heating system and describe how it works.
4. Explain the difference between a passive solar-heating system and an active solar-heating system.
5. Why is fiberglass a good insulating material?
6. Explain how a cooling system works.

Critical Thinking and Problem Solving

Use the skills you have developed in this chapter to answer each of the following.

1. **Making diagrams** Draw a diagram showing how a heat-pump system gathers heat from the outside air and uses this heat to warm air inside a building. Be sure to label your diagram.
2. **Classifying** Classify each of the following central heating systems as direct or indirect: warm air, hot water, steam, heat pump, radiant hot water, solar.
3. **Interpreting photographs** Does the building in the photograph make use of an active solar-heating system or a passive solar-heating system? How can you tell?
4. **Making inferences** Why do you think an alcohol rub might at one time have been used to help a person with a high fever?
5. **Applying concepts** Explain how each of the following insulating materials works: plastic foam used in a picnic cooler; goose down used in a ski jacket; aluminum foil used to wrap hot food for a takeout order.
6. **Making comparisons** Describe how a gasoline engine and a diesel engine are alike and how they are different.
7. **Using the writing process** Pretend that you are James Watt, the eighteenth-century Scottish engineer who is credited with inventing the steam engine. Write a letter to a friend describing your invention and explaining how it works. Include a sketch of your steam engine and some suggestions for practical applications.

GAZETTE

JENEFIR ISBISTER:
SHE DOES DIRTY WORK FOR CLEANER COAL

Jenefir Isbister knelt in the blackened soil outside a Pennsylvania coal mine. With a garden trowel, she scooped some dry black soil into a plastic box. The next day, she dug up some soil from outside a coal-processing plant near the laboratory in which she works. She even scooped up a little mud from the bank of a creek in her own backyard.

Why was Dr. Isbister collecting all this soil? "My boss asked me to find a microorganism to remove sulfur from coal," she explains. And such a microorganism might make its home in coal-rich soil. Dr. Isbister is an expert on microorganisms, or living things that are too small to be seen without special equipment. Microorganisms include a variety of bacteria.

Many microorganisms—often called microbes—feed upon nature's garbage, such as fallen leaves and the remains of dead animals and plants. The microbe that Dr. Isbister was searching for was one that eats the sulfur in coal—a sulfur-eating coal bug.

But why would Isbister be looking for such a thing? As she puts it, "A coal bug could help solve the problem of acid rain." In many parts of the world, acid rain is a serious problem whose effects include the death of trees, fishes, and other living things.

Acid rain is often caused by burning coal that contains high levels of sulfur. The coal smoke produced contains sulfur dioxide. Sulfur dioxide chemically combines with water in the air to form sulfuric acid, a very strong acid. The acid falls to the Earth as acid rain, acid snow, and even acid fog.

One way to reduce acid rain, then, is to remove as much sulfur as possible from the coal. Washing the coal before burning it is the simplest method of scrubbing out the sulfur. But coal washing is expensive and removes only some of the sulfur. Prying more sulfur out of coal requires a chemical reaction—the kind of chemical reaction microbes produce when they dine.

"A sulfur-eating microbe would let us use high-sulfur coal," Dr. Isbister explains. And high-sulfur coal is relatively inexpensive and plentiful.

So Dr. Isbister began collecting soil in the hope of finding a microbe that eats sulfur. "Soil is the best place to look for microorganisms that will grow under many conditions," she explains. "We didn't want bugs we had to baby!"

In the first step of experimentation, Dr. Isbister and Dr. Richard Doyle, a co-worker at the Atlantic Research Corporation in Alexandria, Virginia, crushed each soil sample and placed a small amount of each in separate flasks of salt solution. "The solution keeps the microbes alive while we separate them from the soil," Isbister explains.

A special machine was then used to wash the bugs out of the soil in each flask. Liquid from the top of each flask was then added to another flask filled with nutrient broth. "It's a kind of soup that feeds the microorganisms," explains Isbister.

Next, the researchers added sulfur to each microbe broth. "We did lots of tests. After a long time, we found one solution that contained less sulfur than we had put in," says Isbister. The microbes in this broth had done the best job of eating sulfur. Surprisingly, the sulfur-eating microbes were the ones from her own backyard! Unfortunately, it had taken the microbes 7 days to lower the sulfur level by only 7 percent. "Seven percent is very little; seven days is horrible," says Isbister. "But it was a start. We had a little celebration."

Now the team added powerful chemicals to the broth, hoping to change the microbes' basic metabolism, or cell processes. The goal was to make the microbes even hungrier for sulfur.

"I tested 250 chemical combinations," Isbister recalls. Finally, she found one combination that caused the microbes to eat 80 percent of the sulfur in just 18 hours. "Then we really celebrated, and Dr. Doyle and I applied for a patent on Coal Bug One." Coal Bug One is the nickname the researchers have given their sulfur-eating microbe. Two and one-half years of research had finally resulted in success.

Will Coal Bug One solve the problem of high-sulfur coal? "Coal Bug One eats just one of the many kinds of sulfur found in coal," Isbister replies. "So we'll need to find more bugs. But Coal Bug One is the first step."

▼ Coal Bug One, shown here in an electromicrograph (left), may solve the problem of burning high-sulfur coal (right).

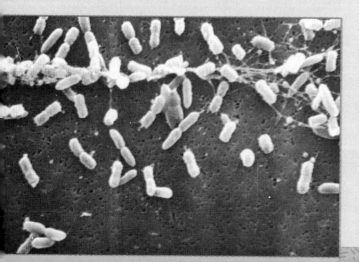

HOTHOUSE EARTH:

Will the Greenhouse Effect Occur?

Imagine a typical urban land-scape with factory chimneys puffing columns of smoke and automobiles exhaling trails of exhaust. Now picture a Chinese countryside dotted with carefully cultivated rice paddies, or an American midwestern grassland covered with herds of peacefully grazing cattle. What do these scenes have in common?

Although they may seem totally different, these scenes actually share a common characteristic. That characteristic has to do with chemistry. Chemical reactions are taking place in the factories, the automobiles, the rice paddies, and even the cattle herds. The types of chemical reactions are different, but they all produce the same byproducts. And these byproducts may be disrupting the Earth's climate by heating the Earth's atmosphere at a rapid rate. This increase in the Earth's temperature is called the greenhouse effect. The gaseous byproducts of industry and agriculture that cause the greenhouse effect are called greenhouse gases. They include carbon dioxide, water vapor, methane, nitrous oxides, and chloro-fluorocarbons (CFCs) used as refrigerants and in aerosol sprays.

The heating process caused by the greenhouse effect is called global warming. When greenhouse gases rise into the atmosphere, they act like a shield of greenhouse glass wrapped around the Earth. That is, they let in sunlight while trapping heat radiated from the Earth. As a result, the atmosphere becomes warmer.

Although scientists may debate the details of the process of global warming, they do agree on some statistics. For example, they

◀ **What do peaceful rice paddies have in common with the factory smokestacks shown on the opposite page? Both may contribute to global warming caused by the greenhouse effect.**

Global warming will probably produce major shifts in world weather patterns, bringing drought to fertile areas and destructive rainfall to fragile deserts. In certain areas, higher winter temperatures will mean more rain and less snow, causing flooding in winter and serious dry spells in summer. Excessive heat may result in crop failures—and thus food shortages—around the world. The Earth's wildlife, unable to adapt quickly enough to changes in climate, will also suffer. Increased temperatures may favor the growth of weeds and insects harmful to various useful plants, which may have difficulty reproducing in warmer climates. Animals will lose their natural habitats as well as precious food and water sources.

Many scientists further fear what they call positive-feedback effects. Positive-feedback effects are the results of global warming that actually reinforce global warming. For example, higher temperatures will cause more water to evaporate from the oceans. This additional water vapor will rise into the atmosphere, where it will contribute to the greenhouse effect and increase the effects of global warming.

"We're conducting a dangerous experiment," says Columbia University geology

▼ **Cities and towns in low-lying areas may be in danger of flooding if sea levels rise as a result of global warming.**

know that the amount of carbon dioxide in the atmosphere is at its highest level ever. That level is 25 percent higher than it was in 1860. Scientists expect the amount of carbon dioxide to double by the middle of the next century if humans continue to pump greenhouse gases into the atmosphere at current rates. They also expect the average global temperature to rise between 1.5°C and 4.5°C by the year 2050.

Such an increase in the average global temperature may appear insignificant at first. It seems more serious, however, when we consider that the Earth's temperature has risen only 5°C over the last 10,000 years! What does such a rapid rise in average global temperature actually mean? Climatologists are trying to answer this question by using sophisticated computer models to study the Earth's climate, past and present, and to predict the future effects of global warming. Many of the effects they anticipate are devastating for the Earth and its people.

One of the most likely results of a warmer Earth is a rise in global sea levels: The expansion of water and the melting of glaciers may cause the oceans to rise from 0.3 to 1.8 meters, resulting in flooding of low-lying coastal areas and islands. Cities such as Miami, Florida, and Galveston, Texas, would be swamped. In countries such as Bangladesh and Egypt, the many cities and towns built around river deltas could be washed away. In addition, higher sea levels will increase the violence and frequency of hurricanes and other severe storms.

▲ **The effects of global warming may be reduced by limiting the production of greenhouse gases. Using the energy of the wind instead of burning fossil fuels may be one answer.**

professor Wallace Broecker. "Yet since it's a necessity for running the world, we go ahead and do it." Indeed, since the beginning of the Industrial Revolution in the 1860s, much of the world has become more and more dependent for everyday life on the chemical reactions that produce greenhouse gases. These reactions include the burning of fossil fuels (coal, oil, and natural gas) for energy to warm our houses and office buildings, to run machines and factories, and to power automobiles and other vehicles. So limiting the production of greenhouse gases goes to the heart of modern industrial life. In fact, putting an end to global warming would require a return to a preindustrial world, if such a thing were possible.

Is there any hope for slowing global warming? Yes, scientists do offer some ways to cut down the production of greenhouse gases and so reduce global warming. Most involve energy conservation: using less coal, burning fossil fuels more efficiently, and seeking alternatives to fossil fuels. Other solutions include ending the massive destruction of tropical rain forests and encouraging

reforestation. Forests are important in the fight against global warming because trees help remove carbon dioxide from the air. Scientists, environmentalists, and concerned citizens also offer another suggestion: teamwork. As the name suggests, global warming is a global problem. As such, all the diverse peoples of the world must come together to solve it.

▼ **Geothermal energy—heat from within the Earth—is another possible alternative to fossil fuels.**

WIRED TO THE SUN

The house of the future will run on energy from the sun, make its own electricity, and even sell some of it to the electric company!

It looks like an ordinary house, nestled among several others just like it. The lights are on in the kitchen. Good—dinner will be ready soon. Let's see . . . what was it you ordered for supper before you left the house this morning? Oh, yes, a menu featuring your favorite Italian dishes. Mmm . . .

POWER PANELS

The thought of collapsing into a comfortable chair in a cool room makes you walk even faster. Not such a good idea on a day that saw the temperature reach 35°C—for the sixth day in a row. The only advantage to this heat wave is that it will enable you to sell back lots of electricity to the power company. Yes, indeed, those 64 solar panels rising up from the southern side of the roof really do their job. They produce enough electricity to run most of the major appliances in the house. The panels, covering a roof area of 5.5 square meters, are made up of *photovoltaic cells*. These cells change the energy in sunlight directly into electricity.

▶ Each one of the 64 solar panels in the roof of this house is made up of photovoltaic cells. These cells capture the energy of the sun and change it directly into electricity.

▲ **Both the trombe wall and the wall containing phase-change salts can be seen in this view of the house. These solar features, designed to get the most out of the sun's natural heating ability, are for winter use only.**

Now, of course, when there is no strong sunlight—during the night and on cloudy days—the photovoltaic cells don't work. But you need not worry. At those times, your house is automatically switched to a local electric company's cables. You use its electricity and pay its prices. But so far this summer, the photovoltaic cells have produced more energy than the house needs. Some of the energy has been stored in the hot-water heater. The remainder has been sold back to the electric power company. The electricity is actually sent from the roof through cables to a nearby company station. Just think of it: The electricity you sell back is used to power one of those old-fashioned houses!

COMPUTER COMFORT

As you climb the stairs to the air-lock entry, you happily notice that the outside window shutters have been automatically rolled down. These shutters reflect sunlight on hot days and help hold heat in the house

on cold days. Shutters inside the windows have also been automatically lowered. Keeping direct sunlight out of the house on a day like today is important.

Punching your code in the door keypad, you walk into the air-lock entry. The air lock keeps hot air from entering the house in summer. In winter, it keeps the cold air out. The burglar-alarm system now shuts itself off. It feels a bit too cool in the house, so you can signal the air-conditioning system to quit working so hard by punching another code into the thermostat.

As you pass from room to room, doors open automatically and lights switch on and off. The heat-and-motion sensors built into the floors, walls, and ceilings keep track of your path. And sure enough, as you enter the family room, your favorite music starts to play.

With dinner cooking in the oven, which automatically went on when you walked in, you can sit down for awhile and relax. The dusting and vacuuming have all been done by the computer-driven robots. The kitchen computer keeps track of what food items you are getting low on. It will "call in" a list of groceries to the supermarket later.

So you're now free to sit and think about just how comfortable your home life is. The main computer of your house-management system takes care of almost everything—from controlling heating and cooling systems to providing news and sports information and educational courses. It opens locks, gives fire-alarm protection, cooks meals, turns lights on and off. It remembers when to turn certain appliances on or off. It even takes readings of the dust level on the solar panels and lets you know when they need washing! Maybe someday soon, the computer will take care of cleaning the photovoltaic cells too!

SOLAR SERVICE

One amazing thing about your house is how well it uses energy. That's because it has several special features. These features are designed to get the most out of the sun's natural heating ability in winter. At the same time, they are designed not to add heat to the house in summer. How can this be done?

That black wall covered with glass along the south side of the house is called a trombe wall. Its job is to collect the sun's rays. When these rays pass through the glass, they strike the trombe wall and are absorbed. The wall is painted black to make sure as much of the sun's energy as possible is absorbed. Dark colors absorb sunlight best. The wall heats up as it absorbs energy. Because the wall is very thick, a great deal of heat is stored. At night or on a cloudy day, that heat is slowly released into the house. The glass covering is about 15 centimeters from the wall and creates an air space. This space prevents the heat from escaping to the outside.

The trombe wall is a wintertime-only feature. During the summer months, the wall is shaded.

Phase-change salts are another amazing solar feature. Along the south side of the house, tubes no longer than 76 centimeters are built into the wall. These tubes are painted black on the outside to absorb the greatest amount of solar energy. Inside the tubes are special calcium compounds, which are solids at temperatures below 27.2°C, their melting point. During the day, the sun's radiation is absorbed by the salts. The salts melt if their temperature goes above 27.2°C. But during the time they melt and stay liquid, they store the sun's heat energy. Then at night, when the temperature drops below the melting point, the salts turn back to the solid phase. This phase change releases the stored heat energy to the house. However, like the trombe wall, the salt-containing tubes must be shaded during the summer months.

Well, these solar features have come a long way since they were first introduced back in the 1970s. Since then, they have been modified and improved. So now in 1997, they help keep your house warm as toast in winter and cool as a cucumber in summer. That thought reminds you that your computer is calling—dinner is ready!

▼ **The large rounded shape in the front of the house is the air-lock entry, which keeps hot air out of the house in summer and cold air out of the house in winter. The automatic shutters that reflect sunlight away in summer can be seen covering the upstairs windows.**

For Further Reading

If you have been intrigued by the concepts examined in this textbook, you may also be interested in the ways fellow thinkers—novelists, poets, essayists, as well as scientists—have imaginatively explored the same ideas.

Chapter 1: What Is Heat?

Adler, Irving. *Hot and Cold: The Story of Temperature From Absolute Zero to the Heat of the Sun*. New York: John Day.

Cobb, Vicki. *Heat*. New York: Watts.

Doolittle, Hilda. *Collected Poems*. New York: AMS Press.

Herbert, Frank. *Dune*. New York: Berkley Publishing.

Pullman, Philip. *The Ruby in the Smoke*. New York: Knopf.

Chapter 2: Uses of Heat

Auel, Jean. *Clan of the Cave Bear*. New York: Crown Publishing.

Bradbury, Ray. *Fahrenheit 451*. New York: Ballantine.

Kavaler, Lucy. *A Matter of Degree: Heat, Life and Death*. New York: Harper.

London, Jack. *The Great Short Works of Jack London*. New York: Harper Collins.

O'Dell, Scott. *Island of the Blue Dolphins*. New York: Dell.

Paulsen, Gary. *Hatchet*. New York: MacMillan/ Bradbury.

Penrose, Gordon. *Sensational Science Activities with Dr. Zed*. New York: Simon & Schuster.

Schneider, Stephen. *Global Warming*. New York: Random House.

Stone, A. Harris, and B. Siegel. *The Heat's On*. Englewood Cliffs, NJ: Prentice Hall.

Taylor, Mildred. *Roll of Thunder, Hear My Cry*. New York: Dial.

Twain, Mark. *Life on the Mississippi*. New York: Airmont.

Wu, William. *Hong on the Range*. New York: Walker Press.

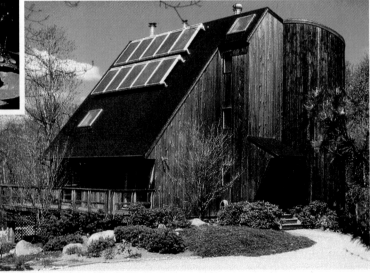

Activity Bank

Welcome to the Activity Bank! This is an exciting and enjoyable part of your science textbook. By using the Activity Bank you will have the chance to make a variety of interesting and different observations about science. The best thing about the Activity Bank is that you and your classmates will become the detectives, and as with any investigation you will have to sort through information to find the truth. There will be many twists and turns along the way, some surprises and disappointments too. So always remember to keep an open mind, ask lots of questions, and have fun learning about science.

MAY THE FORCE (OF FRICTION) BE WITH YOU

When you rub your hands together, they feel warmer. What causes your hands to warm up? The answer is friction. Friction is a common force that resists motion. Friction is caused by one surface rubbing against another surface. In this activity you will measure and compare the force of friction on two different surfaces, one smooth and one rough. Where do you think the force of friction will be greater—on the smooth surface or the rough surface?

Materials

spring scale
small weight
sandpaper
tape

Procedure

1. Attach a small weight to a spring scale. A spring scale measures weight in units called newtons. What is the weight of the object in newtons?

2. Place the weight on a smooth, flat surface, such as a table top. Use the spring scale to pull the weight across the surface of the table. How much force is shown on the spring scale? Subtract the weight of the object from the amount of force shown on the spring scale. The result is the force of friction for the table top. What is this force in newtons?

3. Tape a piece of sandpaper to the table top. Repeat step 2, but this time use the spring scale to pull the weight across the sandpaper. What is the force of friction for the sandpaper? Is the force of friction greater for a smooth surface or for a rough surface? Was your prediction correct?

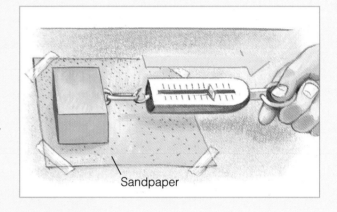
Sandpaper

Do It Yourself

Have you ever used sandpaper to smooth the rough edges of a piece of wood? What happens to the wood when you rub it with the sandpaper? Try it and find out.

Think for Yourself

You may have seen beautifully polished samples of rocks and minerals as part of a display in a museum of natural history. During the grinding and polishing process, water is sprayed onto the rock surface. Based on what you know about friction, why do you think this is done?

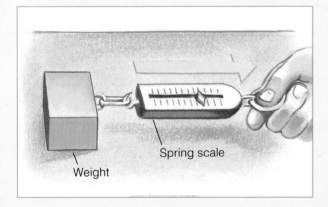
Spring scale
Weight

ONE HUNDRED DEGREES OF SEPARATION

Temperature is measured with a thermometer. All thermometers have a scale, or a set of numbers, that allows you to read the temperature. On a Celsius thermometer, the scale runs from 0°C (the freezing point of water) to 100°C (the boiling point of water). In this activity you will calibrate, or mark the scale on, an unmarked thermometer.

Materials

unmarked thermometer
2 beakers
ring stand and ring
Bunsen burner
ice
glass-marking pencil
metric ruler

Procedure

1. Place the unmarked thermometer in a beaker of water. Heat the water over a Bunsen burner until the water begins to boil. **CAUTION:** *Be careful when using a Bunsen burner.*

2. When the column of liquid in the thermometer stops rising, remove the thermometer from the beaker.

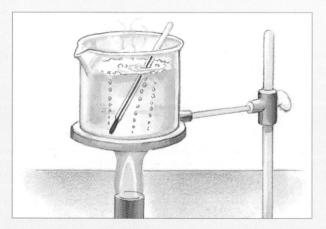

CAUTION: *The thermometer will be hot.* Mark the point at which the liquid stopped rising. What is the temperature at which the liquid rose as high as it would go in the thermometer? Write this temperature next to the mark you made on the thermometer.

3. Allow the thermometer to cool a bit. Then place the thermometer into a beaker of ice water. When the liquid stops falling, remove the thermometer from the beaker. Mark the point at which the liquid stopped falling. What is the temperature at which the liquid fell as low as it would go? Write this temperature next to the mark you just made on the thermometer.

4. Using a metric ruler, divide the space between the high point and the low point into 10 equal parts. Mark these divisions. How many degrees does each mark represent?

Think for Yourself

Suppose you wanted to calibrate your thermometer using the Kelvin scale instead of the Celsius scale. What number would you write next to the highest mark? The lowest mark?

THESE "FUELISH" THINGS

Just as rocket fuel provides the energy needed to launch the Space Shuttle, so the food you eat contains fuel that provides your body with the energy you need every day. This fuel is in the form of stored energy called potential energy. You cannot measure the amount of potential energy in food directly. Instead, you can measure the heat energy, in calories, gained by water when a sample of food is burned. The heat energy gained is equal to the heat energy lost by the burning food.

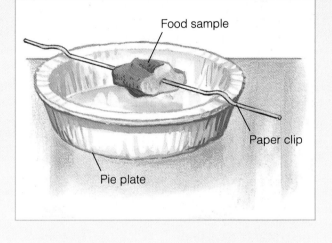

Food sample

Paper clip

Pie plate

Materials

triple-beam balance
assorted food
   samples
   (peanuts, bread,
   and so forth)
flask
matches

ring stand and
   clamp
paper clip
aluminum pie plate
Celsius thermometer
clock or watch

Procedure

1. Find the mass of the empty flask in grams.

2. Half fill the flask with water and find the mass of the flask and the water. Then subtract to find the mass of the water alone. Record this mass in a data table similar to the one shown.

3. Clamp the flask onto the ring stand. Measure and record the temperature of the water (T_i).

4. Carefully straighten the paper clip and stick it through the food sample.

5. Position the paper clip so that the ends rest on the edges of the pie plate.

6. Use a match to ignite the food sample. **CAUTION:** *Be careful when using matches.* Once the food begins to burn, blow out the match and dispose of it safely.

7. Place the pie plate directly below the flask. Let the food burn for 3 minutes and then blow out the flame. Record the temperature of the water as T_f in your data table.

Observations

DATA TABLE

Food Sample	Mass of Water (g)	Temperature (°C)	
		T_i	T_f

Analysis and Conclusions

1. Use the following equation to calculate the heat energy gained by the water in the flask as the food burned:

Heat gained = Mass x Change in temperature x Specific heat

= Mass x (T_f - T_i) x 1 cal/g·°C

2. How much heat energy was lost by the burning food sample? (Remember, heat gained = heat lost.)

3. Share your results with the rest of the class. Make a class data table showing the results for the different food samples tested. Which food sample released the most heat energy? The least?

4. Most of the heat energy lost by the burning food was absorbed by the water in the flask. What might have happened to any heat energy that was not absorbed by the water?

LET THE SUN SHINE IN

How does a passive solar-heating system work? In this activity you will build a simple model to find out. You will need two shoe boxes, plastic wrap, tape, scissors, and two Celsius thermometers.

1. Cut a square "window" at one end of each shoe box.

2. Tape a piece of clear plastic wrap over each window.

3. Place a thermometer inside each box. Be sure that the temperature inside the boxes is the same (near normal room temperature, about 20°C). Then place the lid on each box.

4. Place both shoe boxes in direct sunlight. Position one box so that its window faces the sun. Position the other box so that its window faces away from the sun. Which box do you predict will get warmer? Why?

5. After about 30 minutes, open the boxes and read the temperature on each thermometer. Which shoe box got warmer? Was your prediction correct? Based on your results, how do you think the windows of a house should be oriented to get the most benefit from a passive solar-heating system?

On Your Own

As a class project, you might want to design and build a more elaborate model of a passive solar home. What conditions should you consider when designing your model?

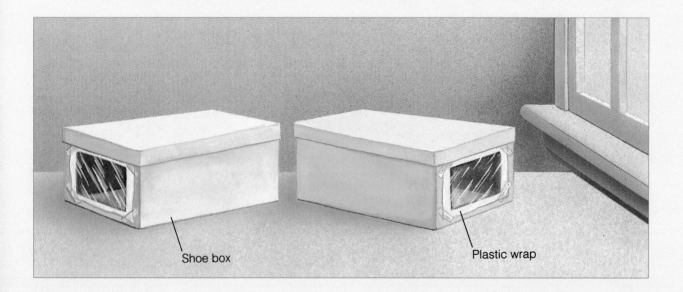

Shoe box

Plastic wrap

TURN DOWN THE HEAT

Most of the energy we use every day comes from fossil fuels—coal, oil, and natural gas. Unfortunately, supplies of fossil fuels on Earth are limited. How can we make supplies of fossil fuels last longer? Most environmentalists recommend using fuel-efficient engines as one way to conserve energy. Another solution is the use of proper insulation for homes and other buildings. The better insulated a building is, the less fuel it will need for heating and cooling. There are many kinds of insulating materials. Which one is the best insulator? Let's find out.

Materials

assorted insulating materials
2 bowls
2 baby food jars
graduated cylinder
2 Celsius thermometers
clock or watch

Procedure

1. Choose a material that you think would be a good insulator. Place a layer of the material in the bottom of a small bowl.

2. Place an empty baby food jar on top of the insulation. Then pack more of the insulation around the sides of the jar.

3. Place a second jar directly into another small bowl. Do not put any insulation around this jar.

4. Carefully fill each jar with the same amount of hot water. **CAUTION:** *Do not use boiling water.*

5. Place a thermometer in each jar and record the temperature of the water as T_i in a data table similar to the one shown.

6. After 15 minutes, record the temperature of the water in each jar as T_f in your data table. To find the change in temperature, subtract T_f from T_i. Record the change in temperature in your data table.

7. Repeat this procedure using different insulating materials.

(continued)

Observations

DATA TABLE

Insulating Material	Temperature (°C)		Temperature Change
	T_i	T_f	

Analysis and Conclusions

1. Which of the insulating materials you tested was most effective in preventing heat loss? How do you know? Is this material currently being used for insulation? If so, where?

2. Do you think any of the insulating materials you tested could be used to insulate buildings? Why or why not?

Going Further

Share your results with the class. Prepare a class data table listing all the different types of insulating materials tested. Which material was the best insulator?

Think for Yourself

1. Suppose you had discovered a new, more efficient insulating material. How would you convince a builder to use this insulation even though it is more expensive than other insulating materials?

2. Do you think the government should encourage private citizens to make better use of insulation in their homes? Why or why not?

The metric system of measurement is used by scientists throughout the world. It is based on units of ten. Each unit is ten times larger or ten times smaller than the next unit. The most commonly used units of the metric system are given below. After you have finished reading about the metric system, try to put it to use. How tall are you in metrics? What is your mass? What is your normal body temperature in degrees Celsius?

Commonly Used Metric Units

Length   The distance from one point to another

meter (m)   A meter is slightly longer than a yard.
               1 meter = 1000 millimeters (mm)
               1 meter = 100 centimeters (cm)
               1000 meters = 1 kilometer (km)

Volume   The amount of space an object takes up

liter (L)   A liter is slightly more than a quart.
               1 liter = 1000 milliliters (mL)

Mass   The amount of matter in an object

gram (g)   A gram has a mass equal to about one paper clip.
               1000 grams = 1 kilogram (kg)

Temperature   The measure of hotness or coldness

degrees   0°C = freezing point of water
Celsius (°C)   100°C = boiling point of water

Metric–English Equivalents

2.54 centimeters (cm) = 1 inch (in.)
1 meter (m) = 39.37 inches (in.)
1 kilometer (km) = 0.62 miles (mi)
1 liter (L) = 1.06 quarts (qt)
250 milliliters (mL) = 1 cup (c)
1 kilogram (kg) = 2.2 pounds (lb)
28.3 grams (g) = 1 ounce (oz)
°C = 5/9 × (°F − 32)

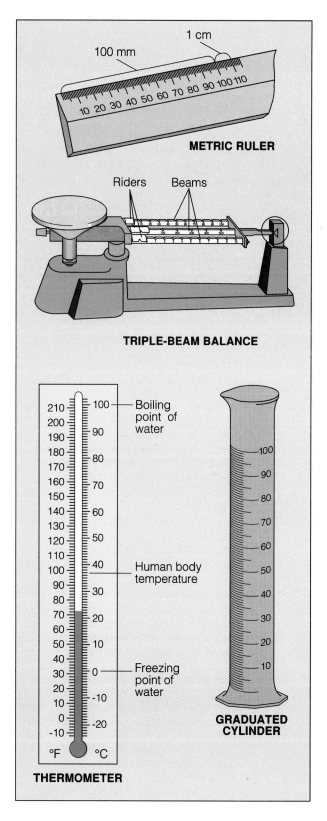

METRIC RULER

TRIPLE-BEAM BALANCE

Riders   Beams

Boiling point of water

Human body temperature

Freezing point of water

THERMOMETER

GRADUATED CYLINDER

Glassware Safety

1. Whenever you see this symbol, you will know that you are working with glassware that can easily be broken. Take particular care to handle such glassware safely. And never use broken or chipped glassware.
2. Never heat glassware that is not thoroughly dry. Never pick up any glassware unless you are sure it is not hot. If it is hot, use heat-resistant gloves.
3. Always clean glassware thoroughly before putting it away.

Fire Safety

1. Whenever you see this symbol, you will know that you are working with fire. Never use any source of fire without wearing safety goggles.
2. Never heat anything—particularly chemicals—unless instructed to do so.
3. Never heat anything in a closed container.
4. Never reach across a flame.
5. Always use a clamp, tongs, or heat-resistant gloves to handle hot objects.
6. Always maintain a clean work area, particularly when using a flame.

Heat Safety

Whenever you see this symbol, you will know that you should put on heat-resistant gloves to avoid burning your hands.

Chemical Safety

1. Whenever you see this symbol, you will know that you are working with chemicals that could be hazardous.
2. Never smell any chemical directly from its container. Always use your hand to waft some of the odors from the top of the container toward your nose—and only when instructed to do so.
3. Never mix chemicals unless instructed to do so.
4. Never touch or taste any chemical unless instructed to do so.
5. Keep all lids closed when chemicals are not in use. Dispose of all chemicals as instructed by your teacher.

6. Immediately rinse with water any chemicals, particularly acids, that get on your skin and clothes. Then notify your teacher.

Eye and Face Safety

1. Whenever you see this symbol, you will know that you are performing an experiment in which you must take precautions to protect your eyes and face by wearing safety goggles.
2. When you are heating a test tube or bottle, always point it away from you and others. Chemicals can splash or boil out of a heated test tube.

Sharp Instrument Safety

1. Whenever you see this symbol, you will know that you are working with a sharp instrument.
2. Always use single-edged razors; double-edged razors are too dangerous.
3. Handle any sharp instrument with extreme care. Never cut any material toward you; always cut away from you.
4. Immediately notify your teacher if your skin is cut.

Electrical Safety

1. Whenever you see this symbol, you will know that you are using electricity in the laboratory.
2. Never use long extension cords to plug in any electrical device. Do not plug too many appliances into one socket or you may overload the socket and cause a fire.
3. Never touch an electrical appliance or outlet with wet hands.

Animal Safety

1. Whenever you see this symbol, you will know that you are working with live animals.
2. Do not cause pain, discomfort, or injury to an animal.
3. Follow your teacher's directions when handling animals. Wash your hands thoroughly after handling animals or their cages.

One of the first things a scientist learns is that working in the laboratory can be an exciting experience. But the laboratory can also be quite dangerous if proper safety rules are not followed at all times. To prepare yourself for a safe year in the laboratory, read over the following safety rules. Then read them a second time. Make sure you understand each rule. If you do not, ask your teacher to explain any rules you are unsure of.

Dress Code

1. Many materials in the laboratory can cause eye injury. To protect yourself from possible injury, wear safety goggles whenever you are working with chemicals, burners, or any substance that might get into your eyes. Never wear contact lenses in the laboratory.

2. Wear a laboratory apron or coat whenever you are working with chemicals or heated substances.

3. Tie back long hair to keep it away from any chemicals, burners and candles, or other laboratory equipment.

4. Remove or tie back any article of clothing or jewelry that can hang down and touch chemicals and flames.

General Safety Rules

5. Read all directions for an experiment several times. Follow the directions exactly as they are written. If you are in doubt about any part of the experiment, ask your teacher for assistance.

6. Never perform activities that are not authorized by your teacher. Obtain permission before "experimenting" on your own.

7. Never handle any equipment unless you have specific permission.

8. Take extreme care not to spill any material in the laboratory. If a spill occurs, immediately ask

your teacher about the proper cleanup procedure. Never simply pour chemicals or other substances into the sink or trash container.

9. Never eat in the laboratory.

10. Wash your hands before and after each experiment.

First Aid

11. Immediately report all accidents, no matter how minor, to your teacher.

12. Learn what to do in case of specific accidents, such as getting acid in your eyes or on your skin. (Rinse acids from your body with lots of water.)

13. Become aware of the location of the first-aid kit. But your teacher should administer any required first aid due to injury. Or your teacher may send you to the school nurse or call a physician.

14. Know where and how to report an accident or fire. Find out the location of the fire extinguisher, phone, and fire alarm. Keep a list of important phone numbers—such as the fire department and the school nurse—near the phone. Immediately report any fires to your teacher.

Heating and Fire Safety

15. Again, never use a heat source, such as a candle or burner, without wearing safety goggles.

16. Never heat a chemical you are not instructed to heat. A chemical that is harmless when cool may be dangerous when heated.

17. Maintain a clean work area and keep all materials away from flames.

18. Never reach across a flame.

19. Make sure you know how to light a Bunsen burner. (Your teacher will demonstrate the proper procedure for lighting a burner.) If the flame leaps out of a burner toward you, immediately turn off the gas. Do not touch the burner. It may be hot. And never leave a lighted burner unattended!

20. When heating a test tube or bottle, always point it away from you and others. Chemicals can splash or boil out of a heated test tube.

21. Never heat a liquid in a closed container. The expanding gases produced may blow the container apart, injuring you or others.

22. Before picking up a container that has been heated, first hold the back of your hand near it. If you can feel the heat on the back of your hand, the container may be too hot to handle. Use a clamp or tongs when handling hot containers.

Using Chemicals Safely

23. Never mix chemicals for the "fun of it." You might produce a dangerous, possibly explosive substance.

24. Never touch, taste, or smell a chemical unless you are instructed by your teacher to do so. Many chemicals are poisonous. If you are instructed to note the fumes in an experiment, gently wave your hand over the opening of a container and direct the fumes toward your nose. Do not inhale the fumes directly from the container.

25. Use only those chemicals needed in the activity. Keep all lids closed when a chemical is not being used. Notify your teacher whenever chemicals are spilled.

26. Dispose of all chemicals as instructed by your teacher. To avoid contamination, never return chemicals to their original containers.

27. Be extra careful when working with acids or bases. Pour such chemicals over the sink, not over your workbench.

28. When diluting an acid, pour the acid into water. Never pour water into an acid.

29. Immediately rinse with water any acids that get on your skin or clothing. Then notify your teacher of any acid spill.

Using Glassware Safely

30. Never force glass tubing into a rubber stopper. A turning motion and lubricant will be helpful when inserting glass tubing into rubber stoppers or rubber tubing. Your teacher will demonstrate the proper way to insert glass tubing.

31. Never heat glassware that is not thoroughly dry. Use a wire screen to protect glassware from any flame.

32. Keep in mind that hot glassware will not appear hot. Never pick up glassware without first checking to see if it is hot. See #22.

33. If you are instructed to cut glass tubing, fire-polish the ends immediately to remove sharp edges.

34. Never use broken or chipped glassware. If glassware breaks, notify your teacher and dispose of the glassware in the proper trash container.

35. Never eat or drink from laboratory glassware. Thoroughly clean glassware before putting it away.

Using Sharp Instruments

36. Handle scalpels or razor blades with extreme care. Never cut material toward you; cut away from you.

37. Immediately notify your teacher if you cut your skin when working in the laboratory.

Animal Safety

38. No experiments that will cause pain, discomfort, or harm to mammals, birds, reptiles, fishes, and amphibians should be done in the classroom or at home.

39. Animals should be handled only if necessary. If an animal is excited or frightened, pregnant, feeding, or with its young, special handling is required.

40. Your teacher will instruct you as to how to handle each animal species that may be brought into the classroom.

41. Clean your hands thoroughly after handling animals or the cage containing animals.

End-of-Experiment Rules

42. After an experiment has been completed, clean up your work area and return all equipment to its proper place.

43. Wash your hands after every experiment.

44. Turn off all burners before leaving the laboratory. Check that the gas line leading to the burner is off as well.

Glossary

Pronunciation Key

When difficult names or terms first appear in the text, they are respelled to aid pronunciation. A syllable in SMALL CAPITAL LETTERS receives the most stress. The key below lists the letters used for respelling. It includes examples of words using each sound and shows how the words would be respelled.

Symbol	Example	Respelling
a	hat	(hat)
ay	pay, late	(pay), (layt)
ah	star, hot	(stahr), (haht)
ai	air, dare	(air), (dair)
aw	law, all	(law), (awl)
eh	met	(meht)
ee	bee, eat	(bee), (eet)
er	learn, sir, fur	(lern), (ser), (fer)
ih	fit	(fiht)
igh	mile, sigh	(mighl), (sigh)
oh	no	(noh)
oi	soil, boy	(soil), (boi)
oo	root, rule	(root), (rool)
or	born, door	(born), (dor)
ow	plow, out	(plow), (owt)

Symbol	Example	Respelling
u	put, book	(put), (buk)
uh	fun	(fuhn)
yoo	few, use	(fyoo), (yooz)
ch	chill, reach	(chihl), (reech)
g	go, dig	(goh), (dihg)
j	jet, gently, bridge	(jeht), (JEHNT-lee), (brihj)
k	kite, cup	(kight), (kuhp)
ks	mix	(mihks)
kw	quick	(kwihk)
ng	bring	(brihng)
s	say, cent	(say), (sehnt)
sh	she, crash	(shee), (krash)
th	three	(three)
y	yet, onion	(yeht), (UHN-yuhn)
z	zip, always	(zihp), (AWL-wayz)
zh	treasure	(TREH-zher)

absolute zero: temperature at which all molecular motion ceases; lowest possible temperature (0 K, –273°C)

active solar-heating system: heating system that uses a solar collector to store heat from the sun and an arrangement of a hot-water heater and pipes to circulate heat throughout a building

bimetallic strip: strip consisting of two different metals that expand at different rates and cause the strip to bend; switch in a thermostat

boiling point: temperature at which a substance changes from the liquid phase to the gas phase

calorie: unit used to measure heat

calorimeter (kal-uh-RIHM-uht-er): instrument used to measure the heat given off in chemical reactions

Celsius scale: metric temperature scale on which water freezes at 0° and boils at 100°

central heating system: system that generates heat for an entire building or group of buildings from a central location

combustion: process in which fuels are combined with oxygen at a high temperature; the burning of a fuel

conduction (kuhn-DUHK-shuhn): heat transfer through a substance or from one substance to another by direct contact of molecules

conductor: substance that transfers heat more easily and rapidly than other substances

convection (kuhn-VEHK-shuhn): heat transfer in liquids and gases by means of convection currents

cooling system: system that removes heat from a building, room, or other enclosed space by evaporation

external-combustion engine: engine in which fuel is burned outside the engine; a steam engine

fiberglass: common insulating material consisting of long, thin strands of glass packed together

freezing point: temperature at which a substance changes from the liquid phase to the solid phase

heat: form of energy caused by the internal motion of molecules of matter

heat engine: machine that changes heat energy into mechanical energy in order to do work

heat of fusion: amount of heat needed to change a substance from the solid phase to the liquid phase

heat of vaporization: amount of heat needed to change a substance from the liquid phase to the gas phase

heat-pump system: heating system that takes heat from the outside air and brings it inside

heat transfer: movement of heat from a warmer object to a cooler one

hot-water system: heating system in which hot water is pumped through pipes to a convector that heats a room by means of convection currents

insulation: prevention of heat loss by reducing the transfer of heat by conduction and convection

insulator: substance that does not conduct heat easily

internal-combustion engine: engine in which the burning of fuel takes place inside the engine; a gasoline engine

Kelvin scale: metric temperature scale on which 0 K represents absolute zero, the freezing point of water is 273 K, and the boiling point of water is 373 K

kinetic (kih-NEHT-ihk) **energy:** energy that a moving object has due to its motion; energy of motion

melting point: temperature at which a substance changes from the solid phase to the liquid phase

molecule (MAHL-ih-kyool): tiny particle of matter that is always in motion

passive solar-heating system: heating system in which a building is heated directly by the rays of the sun

phase change: change of matter from one phase (solid, liquid, or gas) to another

potential (poh-TEHN-shuhl) **energy:** energy stored in a substance

radiant electric system: heating system in which electricity is passed through wires or cables that resist the flow of electricity, thus producing heat

radiant hot-water system: heating system in which hot water runs through a continuous coil of pipe in the floor of a room and heats the room through radiation

radiation (ray-dee-AY-shuhn): heat transfer through space

solar-heating system: heating system that uses the energy of the sun to produce heat

specific heat: ability of a substance to absorb heat energy

steam-heating system: heating system in which steam is forced through pipes from a boiler to a convector that heats a room by means of convection currents

temperature: measure of the motion of molecules

thermal expansion: expansion of a substance due to heat

thermal pollution: damage to the environment due to waste heat that causes an unnatural rise in temperature

thermometer: instrument used to measure temperature

thermostat (THER-muh-stat): device that helps control the temperature in an indoor area or in an appliance

warm-air system: heating system in which heated air is forced through ducts to vents and moves throughout a room by means of convection currents

Index

Credits

Cover Background: Ken Karp
Photo Research: Omni-Photo Communications, Inc.
Contributing Artists: Warren Budd & Assoc., Ltd.; Carol Schwartz/Dilys Evans, Art Representatives; Ray Smith; Ames and Zak; Function Thru Form
Photographs: 4 left: J. Benser/Leo De Wys, Inc.; right: Johnny Johnson/Animals Animals/Earth Scenes; **5** top: NASA; bottom left: Tom Stack/Tom Stack & Associates; bottom right: Rolf Sorensen/Tony Stone Worldwide/Chicago Ltd.; **6** top: Lefever/Grushow/Grant Heilman Photography; center: Index Stock Photography, Inc.; bottom: Rex Joseph; **8** top: Dan McCoy/Rainbow; bottom: Gerhard Gscheidle/Image Bank; **9** left: Colin Bell/Tony Stone Worldwide/Chicago Ltd.; right: P.V.E. Ivory: OUTING/ Mary Evans Picture Library/Photo Researchers, Inc.; **10** and **11** Rebuffat/Photo Researchers, Inc.; **12** Johnny Johnson/Animals Animals/Earth Scenes; **13** Chuck Keeler/Tony Stone Worldwide/Chicago Ltd.; **14** top: Tom Stack/Tom Stack & Associates; bottom: Larry Minden/Minden Pictures,Inc.; **15** Kevin Horan/Stock Boston, Inc.; **16** DPI;**17**J. Messerschmidt/Leo De Wys, Inc.; **18** Leverett Bradley/DPI; **19** top: Craig Tuttle/Stock Market;bottom: Frans Lanting/Minden Pictures, Inc.; **20** Werner Wolff/Black Star; **21** NASA/Omni Photo Communications, Inc.; **23** left: Bill Bachman/Photo Researchers, Inc.; right: Francois Dardelet/Image Bank; **26** left: Ken Karp/Omni Photo Communications, Inc.; right: NASA; **28** top: Geraldine Prentice/Tony Stone Worldwide/Chicago Ltd.; bottom: Luis Castañeda/Image Bank; **29** top: Rolf Sorensen/Tony Stone Worldwide/Chicago Ltd.; bottom left: Randy Duchaine/Stock Market; bottom right: Roy Morsch/Stock Market; **32** Richard Choy/Peter Arnold, Inc.; **33** left: Roy Morsch/Stock Market; right: Jacques Chenet/Woodfin Camp & Associates; **35** Ken Karp; **42** left: Michael Skott/Image Bank; right: Uniphoto; **46** Roy Gumpel/Leo De Wys, Inc.; **47** left: Thomas Braise/Stock Market; right: Harald Sund/Image Bank; **48** J. Benser/Leo De Wys, Inc.; **49** top: Tony Stone Worldwide/Chicago Ltd.; bottom left: Joe Bator/Stock Market; bottom right: Henley & Savage/Stock Market;**50** Al Hamdan/Image Bank; **51** Chris Bonington/ Woodfin Camp & Associates; **52** David Madison Photography; **53** NASA/Science Source/Photo Researchers, Inc.; **54** Hal Clason/Tom Stack & Associates; **55** NASA; **57** Detroit Diesel Corporation; **59** Dan McCoy/Rainbow; **63** Roy Gumpel/Leo De Wys, Inc.; **64** Robert Severi;**65** left: Atlantic Research Corporation; right: Michael Collier/Stock Boston, Inc.; **66** Pete Turner/Image Bank;**67** top: Robert Knight/Leo De Wys, Inc.; bottom:D. Aubert/Sygma; **68** top left: Steve Proehl/Image Bank; top right: Mickey Pfleger/Photo 20–20; bottom: James K. Hackett/Leo De Wys, Inc.; **69** Georgia Power; **70** Robert F. Elliott/ H. Armstrong Roberts, Inc.; **71** Georgia Power; **72** left: Luis Castañ-eda/Image Bank; right: Roy Gumpel/Leo De Wys, Inc; **85** NASA/Science Source/Photo Researchers, Inc.; **87** DPI